Cambridge English Readers

Level 6

Series editor: Philip Prowse

Murder Maker

Margaret Johnson

▨▨ CAMBRIDGE

CAMBRIDGE UNIVERSITY PRESS

Cambridge, New York, Melbourne, Madrid, Cape Town, Singapore,
São Paulo, Delhi, Dubai, Tokyo

Cambridge University Press
The Edinburgh Building, Cambridge CB2 8RU, UK

www.cambridge.org
Information on this title: www.cambridge.org/9780521536639

© Cambridge University Press 2003

First published 2003
6th printing 2010

Printed in the United Kingdom at the University Press, Cambridge

A catalogue record for this publication is available from the British Library

ISBN 978-0-521-53663-9 Paperback
ISBN 978-0-521-68624-2 Paperback plus audio CD pack

Contents

Characters

Carla: a single woman
Diane: Carla's friend
Gemma: Carla's friend
Cathy: Carla's friend
Luis: lives in Cuba
Alec Cartwright: Luis's neighbour
Terry: owns Forest Grange Riding Stables
Pete: Cathy's ex-husband
Ben: Pete and Cathy's son

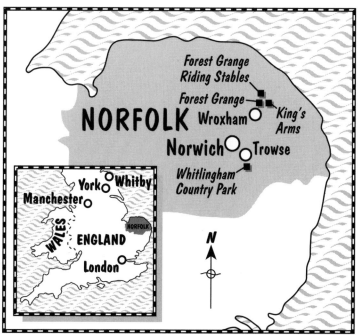

Chapter 1 *The start of it all*

I used to think that murderers were born murderers, but now I know differently. Now I know they can be made.

In my case, it was shock that did it. Four brutal words that changed my life forever. And who spoke those words?

You.

Congratulations, you created a murderer.

But even though I've killed three people, I'm not to blame. You are. Because you betrayed me. And the sad thing is, there's still a part of me that can't believe you did it. Still a part of me that loves you . . .

But don't worry, I'll deal with that. I won't allow a little emotion like love to stop me from killing you. But until then, I'm hoping it will make me feel just a little bit better to write this whole story of sorrow and revenge down. I've got to do something to stop myself from going crazy.

The day you dropped those first seeds of murder into my heart was a hot summer Sunday afternoon in mid-August. August 21, to be precise. Charlotte and Rebecca had escaped from the heat and were indoors in front of the TV, quarrelling about what programme to watch. (No, I didn't hear them quarrelling, but when don't your daughters quarrel?) Anyway, they weren't around. Even the puppy was asleep, lying unconscious on the concrete after a morning of chasing flies. And as for our neighbours, they were all relaxing with the newspapers after their Sunday lunches, content in the knowledge that their gardens were tidy and their cars were shiny and clean.

And you and I? We were lying on a blanket together in the garden. Side by side, in each other's arms beneath my favourite trees. The tall grey poplar trees that marked the boundary of the garden. I loved them for their changing colours, but most of all for their music. They sang and they whispered to us that afternoon, just as they had sung and whispered to us on many other afternoons since I had moved to live in your house.

It's still all so clear in my mind, like a scene from a film. I remember you had your eyes closed and a mixture of shadows and sunshine was painting your face. Your handsome face. Dark, light; dark, light. Shadows, sunshine; shadows, sunshine. Dappled shade, you called it. Dappled shade was your favourite place to be. If we ever had a picnic, you'd say, 'Let's sit in the dappled shade.' And if we went camping, that's where we put the tent, in the dappled shade.

I prefer full sunshine, I must admit, but I never told you that, because what good was sunshine on my own? You and the dappled shade were a million times better to me than full sunshine on my own. You . . . My man. My property. Mine.

I was completely confident of my status as your lifelong partner, lying there beneath the grey poplars. I had no doubt at all that we would be together forever. That we would be walking hand in hand by the sea together after our hair had turned white and your daughters were busy with their own lives. You and me together forever, right up until one of us died. Pathetic, really, especially as you killed me with your words right there in the garden on

August 21. And the worst of it was, there was no warning at all. Nothing to prepare me for those four little words of destruction.

One moment I was lying sleepily next to you under the trees watching the stripes of sunshine painting your face, and the next moment I heard you give a strange, nervous cough.

'Carla,' you said, and something about your voice made me feel instantly afraid.

I remember turning my body towards you and holding my hand to keep the sun out of my eyes. 'What's wrong, darling?' I must have said, or something very similar. Poor, innocent creature. I thought you were ill or something. I was worried about you. 'Tell me, what's wrong, Mark, please!'

Well, you told me. You certainly did.

You looked at me with your beautiful dark eyes and you said, 'I'm sorry, Carla. I'm so sorry. There's no easy way to say this, so I'll just come right out and say it. I . . . I've met somebody else.'

I've been busy in the last twelve months. I've changed my hairstyle. Moved to a new city and started a new job. Had a string of affairs. Some of the sex was even quite good.

I think I was a bit crazy for six months or so. I certainly didn't care very much what happened to me or what I did. So I did pretty much whatever I wanted. Anything I thought might limit the pain. And sometimes it even worked for a short time.

Then one rainy morning I woke up next to some man I'd met in a nightclub the previous evening and I couldn't even remember his name. There was an empty bottle of vodka on the bedside table and my headache was so bad I knew I was responsible for drinking at least half of it. I went to the bathroom, and when I looked at my reflection in the mirror I didn't like what I saw. My face was as white as a ghost's, and there were black circles beneath my eyes. I looked wild and out of control.

And, worst of all, I knew that all the time I was suffering, you were with another woman. I doubted whether you even thought about me any more at all. Suddenly, as I stood there looking at my reflection in the bathroom mirror, the injustice of everything hit me right in the stomach like a hard punch. I had loved you with all my heart, and in return you had stamped me into the dust.

After I'd thrown the stranger out of my bed and out of my flat, I stood under the shower with the water mixing with my tears until the water ran cold. Then, as I dried my shivering body, I decided that enough was enough. I couldn't go on like this. I had to do something to make me feel better, and drinking vodka and spending time with anonymous men clearly wasn't working.

A few weeks earlier I'd seen an advert in the newspaper for a special course for people who have experienced a broken relationship. It was a Restart Course. I dialled the number in the advert, and two weeks later I was sitting in a classroom for the first session. And that's where I met Diane, Gemma and Cathy. Let me tell you, they're worth at least a hundred of you and for the moment they're my family. Or the only family that counts. Let me introduce them.

First up there's Diane, fifty-two, brutally rejected by her husband of twenty-five years in an email from Cuba. Then there's Cathy, thirty-two, abandoned by her husband after several years of depression. Next there's Gemma, forty-five, who made her escape from a twenty-year marriage to a man who cruelly abused her. And then there's me. Carla, thirty-five, replaced by a blonde business studies teacher you met on holiday while I was at home loyally looking after your daughters.

After the weekly Restart class, the girls and I always go to the pub next to the college to have a few drinks and to laugh away some of the tension. And later on we inevitably start to remember happier times.

'My Alec and I used to have such fun when we were first together. Got into trouble all the time.' That's Diane. Long blonde hair, loud laugh. Turning heads left, right and centre even though she's old enough to be Cathy's mother. 'One night on our honeymoon, we decided to make love outdoors. Exciting and romantic, you know. Anyway, we'd just taken our clothes off when a group of elderly walkers came round the corner! I don't know who was more embarrassed, them or us!'

Diane tried to kill herself earlier this year with a combination of alcohol and headache pills. Fortunately she was discovered before it was too late, but she was seriously ill for some time. And Alec, the father of their three daughters, didn't even bother to get up from beneath his Cuban beauty to find out how she was.

Diane, Gemma and Cathy. I've hardly known them any time at all, but somehow I feel I've known them forever. If a life can be so completely changed in the space it takes someone to say four short words, then the whole idea of time means nothing anyway.

'He sent me another charming email from Havana

today,' Diane continues. 'He's disputing my solicitor's claim that I should receive half his pension.'

'The horrible man!' Gemma exclaims, and then she goes on to tell us about a story she read in the newspaper that day about a woman who took revenge on her cheating husband.

'His hobby was collecting valuable wine,' she told us. Gemma's really pretty, and she's gradually becoming more confident now she's got rid of her horrible husband. 'Anyway, his wife was so angry with him she went right round their village leaving bottles of his wine outside people's houses!'

We all laughed, me especially. I could just imagine how satisfying it must have been for that woman, getting rid of all her husband's precious wine. So, a little later on in the evening when Cathy told us all she was thinking of going away on holiday, Gemma's story and the idea of a holiday connected in my mind.

Revenge. Holiday. After the way you'd treated me, I deserved a holiday. And why not go to Cuba? It was a country you'd always wanted to visit. If you ever found out I'd been there before you, you'd be sick with jealousy. Yes, it would be a kind of revenge in a way, to go there first. Not as extreme as the wine story of course, but it would be a start. Yes, I could view it as a first step, a practice for some sort of serious revenge. I could spend my time in Cuba planning what to do to you. Or perhaps better still, I could practise first on someone else . . .

So I turned towards Diane and said casually, 'I'm going on holiday to Cuba next month. Do you want me to pay your husband a visit?'

Chapter 2 *Whispers and echoes*

I experienced Havana through your eyes. No, that doesn't express it properly. It wasn't an intellectual thing at all. I didn't think, 'Mark would have liked this,' or, 'Mark would have done that.' It was more as if I became you. As if your spirit possessed me in some strange way, making me respond to my surroundings the way you would.

The dilapidated Havana streets are alive with shady characters. Especially Old Havana, or Habana Vieja, as it's called in Spanish. The streets of Habana Vieja are no place for a foreign woman to walk alone after dark, I can tell you. Or probably even during the day for that matter. But the very first night I was in Havana, I left the normal tourist routes far behind and wandered past the near-ruined houses along dark streets, and I wasn't afraid. I walked tall with my shoulders back, all my senses working overtime as they absorbed the unique mixture of sights and sounds that is a real Havana night.

Tourists mostly experience a Cuba with its Sunday-best clothes on. A poor but cheerful country where everybody smiles constantly and tries their very best to please you. In a country where a tour guide earns more than a doctor, I suppose this isn't very surprising. Certainly, behind every smiled welcome there's a hunger. They want your money, but they're very polite about it. It's not the same as when we went on holiday to India and we had crowds of beggars running after us.

No, Cuban people are prepared to be nice to you in order to get their hands on your dollars. It's only when you examine those smiles a little more closely that you begin to see how false they are. Really they're jealous of you, with your expensive watch, designer sunglasses and, above all, your passport and freedom to travel. In a country where the supermarket shelves are often almost empty, a tourist is like a precious jewel in a pile of dusty stones.

The real Havana is a city of whispers and echoes. You'd love it, you really would. Lovers kiss in dark passages while music drifts in the humid winds. Paint peels from the front of once-grand buildings and men sit in doorways smoking cigars and drinking rum. And of course there are all the wonderful old cars left over from the days when Hollywood stars visited the city in the 1950s before the Revolution. Cadillac cars sail along the streets, curiosities from another time, polluting the atmosphere as they go. Money that could be spent on clothes or food is spent on cars by people with nowhere to go and nothing to do. Havana is a city populated by people waiting for something to happen.

And, as I walked along the dark streets of Habana Vieja, carrying the spirit of you inside me, many of the people sitting in doorways decided that I might be what they were waiting for. An opportunity.

They used the traditional Cuban way to attract my attention: by making a sound that isn't quite a whistle or a shout, but a strange hiss like a water bird on a lake. And some of the younger men found the energy to get up from their steps to follow me, bringing the smell of cigars and rum along with them.

'Hey, *señorita*! Where are you going? *Señorita*! You are very beautiful!' And somehow, perhaps because I was away from the regular tourist routes, their smiles seemed more genuine than usual.

Was I in danger? I honestly don't know. I'm not even sure I cared very much. Oh, I suppose I didn't really want any actual harm to come to me, but since losing you I have been very aware of how unpredictable life can be. Of how at risk and vulnerable we are all the time. The dark streets of Habana Vieja just didn't seem any more or less dangerous than anywhere else, that's all.

Anyway, I was alone in those unpredictable Havana streets for a reason. Alec Cartwright was renting a room somewhere near to where I was; I had his address in my pocket, written by Diane on a piece of expensive notepaper. But it would be no use going straight round there to challenge him. After all, what would I say? What would I do? No, I needed time to observe him, time to find out about his habits and his way of life. That way I could identify any weak spots which could form the basis of my revenge plans. (You see, I wasn't thinking of murder then, only of some sort of simple revenge.)

But in order to study Alec Cartwright, I needed to find myself a base. Somewhere close to where he lived.

Fortunately, luck was on my side. Suddenly, in the dull light from an antique streetlamp, I saw a card in the front window of a tired-looking house. The card was stained brown by age or damp or possibly both. Of course it was written in Spanish, but it was simple Spanish, and my command of the language was sufficient to understand it. 'Room to rent. Apply Bar Escorpión.'

14

I found the bar right at the end of the street. If I tell you it matched the houses around it, then you'll probably guess that the paint on the walls was faded and peeling and that the metal sign was rusty. It certainly seemed highly unlikely that any tourists had ever passed through its doors before, but I didn't care. I walked in, and I wasn't even put off when a quick glance around the dark interior of the bar revealed territory that was strictly male.

You'd have loved it, I'm sure, because it was straight out of one of those cowboy films you've got such a passion for. I don't know why, they all seem the same to me. Or at least, they all start the same way: a stranger arrives in a sleepy town, gets off his horse, beats the dust from his clothes with his hat and walks into the bar. As the doors close behind him, everyone stops talking . . .

Well, I didn't have a horse and my clothes weren't dusty, but just like in those films, all conversation stopped when I walked in. But I just gave a general smile around the room at everybody, then I went up to the bar and ordered a beer. By the time I'd been served and had settled myself at an empty table in a corner, the conversations had started up again. I guessed that most people were probably talking about me, but I simply chose not to be concerned about it. I didn't care. It wasn't important.

I suppose my desire for revenge had given me a real sense of purpose. But, looking back, I think at that moment in time, I actually felt quite relaxed. After a while I intended to ask about the room, but there was no hurry. There was plenty of time to just sit and drink my beer. Who knew? Perhaps Alec Cartwright himself would come in for a neighbourly chat before supper.

But when the doors did open a few minutes later, it was to admit a man who was the very opposite in looks to the grey-bearded fifty-year-old in the photograph Diane had lent me before I left England. The man filling the doorway had skin like milk chocolate and a smile that spread sunshine to all who received it. And it was only a matter of seconds before I was on the receiving end of some of that warming sunshine.

Luis – for I soon discovered that was his name – walked straight up to my table and sat himself down in the empty seat opposite me. For a while he said absolutely nothing, just looked at me, studying every millimetre of my face. Then a glass of rum arrived as if by magic on the table in front of him. He put his head on one side and picked the drink up.

'I am a reader of faces,' he stated grandly. 'Do you want me to tell you what your face says to me?'

'Well,' I said, impressed by the standard of his English, 'it appears to tell you my nationality anyway.'

Instantly he smiled, and I noticed there was a gap between his front teeth. 'No, your guidebook told me that,' he said, his eyes sparkling, and I smiled back at him, remembering that my *Rough Guide to Cuba* was sticking out of the top of my shoulder bag, which I'd hung from my chair.

'You are English,' he went on, still looking carefully at my face, 'and you have only been in Cuba for a few days.'

'Because I haven't got a suntan, right?' I guessed, and once again that gap-toothed smile shone out at me.

'Yes,' he agreed. 'Because your skin is still pale.'

By now I was enjoying myself. I'd almost forgotten about Alec Cartwright and the true reason I was here.

'Tell me something a little less obvious,' I encouraged him, but immediately regretted it when his face grew more thoughtful.

'You're looking for something or someone,' he said slowly, and suddenly it wasn't a game any longer. 'It's very important that you find him,' he said. 'A person's life depends on it . . .'

The room seemed suddenly cold despite the humid air drifting in through the open windows, and I shivered, avoiding his eyes.

Of course he noticed my tension. 'Am I right?' he asked casually, and I remember how exposed I felt. My new confidence had abandoned me.

But with a huge effort I managed to keep my feelings from my face, or at least I think I did. 'There's an element of truth in that statement,' I said, but if I'd hoped to confuse Luis by using long words, then I was quickly disappointed. His command of the English language was astonishingly good.

'Why don't you tell me all about it?' he suggested.

Of course I wasn't about to betray my plans to a total stranger, even one as attractive and friendly as Luis. Not that I had a plan, beyond finding Alec Cartwright and making him sweat. You see, even then I didn't know just what I was capable of. I suspected I was capable of blackmail, and of inflicting emotional pain, perhaps even severe emotional pain. But I had no suspicion of that potential for violence living just beneath my skin. A potential that was swelling and increasing every second, like undiscovered cancer cells.

'I'm here to do a favour for a friend,' I said. 'She wants me to find a missing reptile.'

For the first time Luis's mind didn't quite connect with the meaning of my words. 'Has your friend lost a snake in Havana?' he asked, and I laughed out loud.

Luis looked slightly offended, so I quickly apologised. 'Actually,' I said, 'you're almost right. She's lost her husband, and I gather he is something of a snake.'

'I see,' Luis said. 'And what is his name, this snake husband of your friend?'

'Alec,' I told him. 'Alec Cartwright.'

And then suddenly it was Luis's turn to laugh.

'What?' I asked him, curious. 'What's so amusing?'

'Alec Cartwright is my neighbour,' he explained finally. And that's when I came to the conclusion that fate must be on my side. It wasn't coincidence that had brought me into this bar at the same time as Alec Cartwright's neighbour, it was fate.

Someone somewhere intended me to get my revenge. It was almost as if I was an actress in a play, speaking the lines of a writer's plot. The situation was out of my control.

And every bit as inevitable as night following day.

Chapter 3   *Mr Mouthwash*

I bought Luis another drink. 'Tell me about Alec Cartwright,' I said.

Luis looked at me, and suddenly his expression was very Cuban. There was a sort of measuring look on his face, and I could almost see his mind thinking, 'What's in this for me? How can I turn this situation to my advantage?' Then he asked me casually. 'What is it that you want to know?'

'Everything there is to know,' I replied, equally casual.

Luis pulled an expressive face. 'Alec Cartwright is fat and his clothes are too small,' he said, his voice full of disgust. 'His big white belly hangs over his trousers, and his neck is purple and tired like the neck of a turkey. The man is ugly. Ugly.' He almost spat the word at me across the table. 'But worst of all,' he went on, 'are his eyes. Alec Cartwright has small, suspicious eyes, and he never looks into your face when he speaks to you.' He paused then, I think to give his last words emphasis. 'I would not trust a man like that if he and I were the only two men left alive on this planet.'

I hadn't been impressed when Diane had first shown me that photograph, I have to admit, but the picture Luis was painting was even more unappealing. It was certainly difficult to imagine that this was the same man who had made love to Diane outdoors on their honeymoon. In fact, the very idea made me shiver.

I'd put the photograph Diane had lent me inside my

Rough Guide to Cuba to keep it safe. Now I took it out and showed it to Luis. 'Is this the same man?' I asked him.

He took the photograph from me and immediately nodded. 'Yes,' he said, his face screwed up with disgust, 'that's him. He is older than that, and uglier. But it's him.'

He returned the photograph to me and I replaced it inside my book, thoughtfully. Maybe Alec Cartwright had changed considerably with age. Maybe it's just something that's inevitable, something that happens to everybody. Even you. Maybe if you lived to the age of fifty your muscles wouldn't be firm any longer. Perhaps you'd be fat too. And bald. But as it is, none of that is going to happen. You'll die a handsome man. I'm doing you a favour, really.

Anyway, back in that Havana bar, Luis was continuing with his story about Alec Cartwright. It was around eleven o'clock in the evening by then, and the room was full of chat and cigar smoke. But somehow, although we were surrounded by people, I was only really aware of Luis. It was almost the same as the effect you had on me when we first met at that party.

'However, despite all these things,' Luis was saying, 'I wasn't surprised when Alec managed to get a Cuban girlfriend. The man wears dull clothes, it is true. He does not look like a rich man and he lives here in these streets instead of in an expensive tourist hotel. But he travels around the city in taxis and he sits in bars drinking cocktails. No, I was not surprised about his girlfriend. But I am surprised when you sit here and you tell me that he has a wife in England who is concerned about him.' Luis shook his head in disbelief. 'The man is an animal with the habits of an animal,' he said. 'Every day he rises at five in the morning. Every day at five in the morning he uses his bathroom, and you understand the pipes in these houses are very old. When somebody uses the water, the pipes they knock and bang about like builders on a building site. My work is mostly at night, and for this reason I normally go to bed one hour before Alec Cartwright gets up. And as soon as I go to sleep, those pipes they wake me up again. And after I'm awake, I lie in bed and I have to listen to him in his bathroom. Every day he uses a mouthwash. And every day I lie there and I have to listen to that mouthwash bubbling around in his throat. How is it possible for someone to make so much noise with a mouthwash, can you tell me that? I tell you it is the sound of the devil!'

Luis's voice was very loud by now, and I became aware that people were looking in our direction. All other conversations in the bar had stopped. And Luis hadn't finished yet.

'Every day I wish for Alec Cartwright to move away. To pack his tight, dusty clothes into his suitcase with his mouthwash and disappear!'

At that, Luis picked up his glass and drank the rest of his rum in one swallow, his handsome face looking dangerous. I wondered what work took him away regularly at night. And I wondered too what he would do to anyone who really annoyed him when just the thought of Alec Cartwright's mouthwash could make him look so fierce.

Then the next moment, he was smiling at me and the tension was lifting from his face. 'You know, Carla,' he said, 'these old Havana buildings, they are full of insects. We Cubans learn to ignore them most of the time. They are familiar to us, you understand, a part of our

21

environment and our day-to-day lives. But some insects they are too unpleasant to ignore. Alec Cartwright is such an insect. The worst type of ugly, stinging insect. And if you say to me that you want to persuade him it is a good idea to return to England to the arms of your friend, then I will do anything in my power to assist you. In fact, it would be my very great pleasure.'

And that's how I ended up staying in Luis's apartment as his guest. And no, I don't suppose I would have accepted his invitation if he hadn't been a young, attractive man. But he was attractive. Very attractive. And charming. Interesting too. We sat together on his sofa and talked about everything. England, Cuba, politics, art . . . I even told him about you. (I think he placed you in the same category as Alec Cartwright: an insect – ha, ha!) And yes, we kissed. Of course. As I said, Luis was a very attractive and charming man. But then, before things could go any further, there was a loud noise from next door.

'Alec Cartwright!' Luis announced crossly, moving away from me slightly. 'He has returned and now he makes preparations for bed.'

'Is that really the pipes making all that noise?' I asked, and Luis nodded.

'Yes, indeed, that is the pipes. But you are fortunate. He does not use the mouthwash at night.'

Soon after that, Luis changed into black trousers and a black shirt and left for work, telling me to make myself at home in his apartment. Alone, I looked around properly for the first time. There was nothing expensive in the apartment, but it definitely had style. Unfortunately however, nothing could disguise the smell of the damp coming from the walls, and later, when I climbed into his bed, the sheets felt chilly.

Not surprisingly, I couldn't get to sleep straight away. The pillows held the smell of Luis's aftershave. It was a nice smell: sexy, like Luis. But somehow it made me think about you. About your smell. The bare skin of your shoulder beneath my cheek as you held me in your arms after love-making. The smooth, soft place behind your ears. The warm hollow of your throat.

Gemma has a theory about smell. She thinks it's the basis of what makes you fall in love with somebody. That if someone doesn't smell right for you, then you'll never fall in love with them. She's probably right.

Anyway, lying in Luis's bed surrounded by Luis's smell, I thought about you and I felt more sad and alone than I had for weeks. But I refused to allow myself to cry. Since the split I'd cried enough tears for a lifetime. Enough tears to know that crying changes nothing. You and your special smell were gone from me forever, and I just had to accept that and deal with it. Which was precisely why I was here in Havana – to deal with it. Or rather to practise dealing with it. Because by the time I'd found ways to get revenge for Diane and then Gemma and Cathy, I would be an expert. And then I would be ready to take my revenge on you.

After that alarming noise from the pipes, there were no more sounds from Alec Cartwright's apartment, and I finally drifted off to sleep. I didn't even wake up properly when Luis came back from work. But when the pipes started up again I found myself lying in Luis's arms, with his face pressed into my hair and his chest against my back, and when Luis swore in Spanish, I could feel the movement of his lips. I shivered, and Luis pulled me closer to him, wrapping his arms around me from behind. It felt comforting somehow, and despite the sound of the pipes, I found myself slipping into a light sleep.

But I woke up again immediately when Alec Cartwright started to use his mouthwash, and it wasn't only because Luis gave a groan of despair. It really was a ridiculously loud noise for an activity taking place on the other side of the wall. A detailed sort of noise, somehow. Certainly it was possible to imagine the liquid of the mouthwash moving around every one of Alec Cartwright's yellow teeth. (I didn't know then that his teeth were yellow of course, but it seemed inevitable, considering the lack of care he appeared to take with the rest of his body.)

Luis sat upright in bed, swearing loudly in Spanish. Then he threw a book at the wall. It landed face down on the floor, and I noticed it was my *Rough Guide to Cuba*. Alec Cartwright's photograph came to rest on the carpet next to Luis's black leather shoes, and the face in the photograph seemed to stare back at us stubbornly. 'I'll use my mouthwash when I want to and for as long as I want to!' it seemed to say.

'Are the walls in these buildings thin?' I asked Luis when at last the sounds from next door had stopped, and he ran an annoyed hand through his black hair, swinging his long legs out of the bed.

'No,' he said, 'they are not thin. But all the buildings in Havana are full of cracks and holes. Perhaps the sound travels through these holes. Or through the pipes. I don't know. It is just another mystery of this city. I will make us some coffee.' He put on a black dressing gown and went into the kitchen, and soon the delicious smell of strong coffee reached my nostrils.

According to my watch, it was only five thirty in the morning, but I doubted whether I would get back to sleep again. There was too much to think about. Luis, for example. What had he been doing for half the night?

'Here,' he said, handing me a steaming mug of coffee, and as he leant across the bed to give it to me, his dressing gown fell open, revealing a long scar down the length of his chest. He saw me looking at it.

'I used to be a bad boy,' he told me.

'Aren't you a bad boy any more?' I asked.

He drank some of his coffee. 'No, not any more,' he said, and smiled. 'Well, not often, anyway.'

Bad boy or not, I knew I had nothing to fear from Luis. In fact, I felt very safe as I sat in bed drinking coffee with him. Safe and protected. 'So, what has your friend told you about her husband?' Luis asked.

'He's a doctor,' I told him. 'He's a doctor and he's here to do a piece of research into why your medical services are so good when your country is so . . .' I broke off, realising just in time that what I'd been about to say was hardly tactful. But Luis supplied the missing word from my sentence anyway.

'Poor,' he said. 'It's OK; you can say it. I will not be offended. Cuba is poor.'

I was embarrassed. 'Yes, well, apparently he was only supposed to be here for six months, but his contract was extended.'

'Perhaps the doctor is taking his time with his research,' Luis suggested.

'You mean on purpose?'

He nodded. 'Of course. Gina is a very beautiful girl.' He gestured with his hands to draw the outline of a woman in the air.

'Gina? That's his girlfriend?'

'Yes. She is twenty-three years old. A nurse at the hospital. She had a Cuban boyfriend until Mr Mouthwash arrived.'

'Mr Mouthwash! That's funny!' I started to laugh, and when Luis laughed too, I found myself thinking what a nice laugh he had. Deep and dark. Extremely sexy. Yours was always a bit boyish for my taste really. A silly schoolboy laugh. Though I loved it of course, because it was yours, a part of you. But it didn't make my knees go weak. You only had to look into my eyes to make me melt, but I can't remember your laugh ever making me tremble with desire.

Luis's laugh came from deep inside his chest, and somehow I found myself reaching out to stroke that chest as it moved, my fingers drawing a line down the length of his scar and across his muscles. And suddenly he wasn't laughing any more, and when I looked up into his face, he was looking down at me seriously. Then he bent to kiss me, and desire swept through my body like a tide. And I doubt whether either of us would have heard if Alec Cartwright had decided to use his mouthwash again.

Chapter 4 *Playing detective*

By nine o'clock that morning I was sitting on a bench outside a park, close to the medical building where Alec Cartwright was based. It was still slightly too early for the tourists to have found their way out of their hotels, so no Cubans had asked me whether I wanted a taxi, a guide, a ticket for La Tropicana or a date for that night.

I had a date, anyway. The key to Luis's apartment was secure in the back pocket of my shorts, and he had promised me dinner that evening. And before that we were meeting for coffee at eleven o'clock this morning.

Luis had gone back to sleep after we'd made these arrangements, and that's where I'd left him, lying peacefully in bed, unaware of the shouts of the children on their way to school beneath his apartment window. By the way, there's an enthusiasm about children in Cuba. They don't drag their feet and quarrel with each other all the way to school, the way your daughters do. And they certainly don't get a lift to school and back.

Anyway, back to Luis. I'd spent enough time with him by then to realise that he was a complex man, one moment relaxed and smiling, the next tense and angry. He was unpredictable, and possibly even slightly dangerous when there was a need for him to be. I doubted whether anyone really knew him. He was the type to always keep a part of himself hidden, perhaps even from himself. Time spent in his company certainly wouldn't be boring, and I was confident we could stay on good terms for as long as my business with Alec Cartwright took.

I yawned and stretched, keeping my eyes fixed on the plain grey medical building on the other side of the road. The musical song of a tocororo bird reached my ears from the small park behind my seat. Brightly coloured Cadillacs smoked past every now and then on the road in front of me. A bicycle taxi. A red, white and blue flash of colour as the tocororo flew away. A group of young Cuban women passed by, dressed in tight T-shirts and short skirts and carrying shopping bags.

I smiled at them, and they smiled back before walking on, chatting to each other in voices every bit as musical as the song of the tocororo bird. I stretched and yawned, the smile still on my face. My body felt tired after the previous night's activities, but it was a pleasant sort of tiredness and even though I'd hardly had any sleep, my mind was alert. Which was just as well, because at that moment a taxi pulled up outside the medical building and a man got out.

Grey hair, small beard, tight white shirt stretched over a huge belly. It could only be Alec Cartwright. Then I realised that he wasn't alone. Someone else was getting out of the taxi. A young Cuban woman in a nurse's uniform. She could only be Gina. Luis had been right; she was beautiful. And young.

The taxi drove away, and the couple stood and kissed each other right there on the pavement. It wasn't a quick kiss either. No, this kiss was deep and passionate, the kiss of lovers who regret the time apart that work makes necessary.

Finally they broke apart. They spoke a few words to each

other before Alec gave the girl a final squeeze and went into the grey building. Gina waited until he had completely disappeared from sight, then walked quickly off up the street. I guessed Alec Cartwright would be working inside until at least lunchtime, so I got off my bench, deciding to follow Gina. I wanted to find out more about the girl he had abandoned Diane for.

She had a good figure, at least what I could see of it from behind. Her legs were long and her waist was tiny, and she walked with a sort of confident rhythm, swinging her hips. I could imagine her being an excellent dancer, and I wondered if Alec Cartwright ever took her dancing. It seemed unlikely.

Up ahead, I saw a sign for the hospital. That's why she's hurrying, I thought; she's late for work. But then, to my surprise, she turned down a narrow side street to the right, away from the hospital. I followed her, keeping my distance, and found myself in a dark street of tall, old apartment buildings. It took a while for my eyes to adjust, but I thought I saw the girl look at her watch, and then her pace increased again. She was obviously late for something, but if it wasn't work, then what was it?

I soon found out. Just as I was starting to think I might lose her, she stopped suddenly to knock on a door. Instantly I slowed down, taking my guidebook out of my bag to make myself look like a tourist. But I needn't have bothered. Gina was knocking on the door again and looking up towards a rusty metal balcony on the third floor. Far from noticing me, she wasn't even aware that I existed.

'Carlos!' I heard her shout, and by then I was near

enough to get a good look at her face, framed as it was by her curly black hair. It was lovely. Young and fresh with a beautiful bone structure and dark eyes. The only thing that spoiled it slightly was her anxious expression, but this disappeared as soon as the window behind the balcony opened and a dark male head looked out.

'Carlos!' Gina smiled immediately, and the man smiled back.

'Gina, *mi amor*!' he called sweetly and threw down a key to her.

Gina waved up at him, giving a laugh which made her sound like one of the excited school children I'd heard earlier that day. Then she picked the key up from the dusty road, and used it to let herself into the apartment building and the arms of her waiting lover. For it was perfectly obvious to me that Carlos was her lover, and not a friend or a brother.

Well, I thought, Alec's got a rival. Well, well, well.

There were no convenient cafés in the dark street, and I didn't particularly fancy waiting in one of the doorways until Gina had finished with Carlos. I would only draw attention to myself if I did. Anyway it was almost ten o'clock, and I was meeting Luis at eleven. So I walked slowly back the way I'd come, the picture of Gina's lovely face turned up towards the window fixed in my mind. Diane's an attractive woman too, believe me. She takes very good care of her appearance, visiting the beauty salon every week and she always wears expensive, stylish clothes. You'd definitely approve of her taste in clothes. You'd like her sense of humour too. And her intelligence.

But if you had to choose between a fifty-two-year-old

woman or a beautiful twenty-three-year-old, you'd do exactly what Alec had done and choose the twenty-three-year-old, wouldn't you? Of course you would. I know you would. My replacement was ten years younger than me, after all.

As I walked back the way I had come, I thought how unfair it was. I knew that Diane had supported, loved and encouraged Alec for all of their married lives. And she had given birth to their daughters. The only crime she had committed was to obtain a few age lines on her well-cared-for face. Lines that reminded Alec Cartwright that he wasn't a young man any longer each time he looked at them.

I wondered whether Alec's conscience ever bothered him. Whether he ever thought of Diane as he was making love to Gina. If there was a corner of his mind that regretted how much he had hurt her. Is there a corner of your mind that regrets how much you hurt me? How much you used me? Probably not. I think you're probably just like Alec Cartwright. I think you've conveniently forgotten just how good I was to you.

A bus went past in a cloud of polluting black smoke, and I looked at my watch. It was still a little too early to meet Luis, but I decided to head for the café we were to meet in anyway, in case it took me a while to find it. So I got out my map and set off on foot, doing my best to absorb myself in the grand but faded architecture of the buildings I was passing. My bitterness and anger was going to come in useful later on when I was serving up revenge, but I didn't want it to spoil my entire visit to Cuba.

In the end, I found the café quite easily, so I ordered a coffee and settled down with my guidebook. The book fell open at an article about Santería, one of the religions practised in Cuba. It's related to African religions, and it involves things like sacrificing chickens to keep the gods happy. People who follow the religion dress all in white, and I'd seen a few of them around Havana. As I read the article, it reminded me of black magic, and in particular the practice of making an image of your enemy for the purposes of revenge. A doll or effigy. Very interesting.

Sitting at a table by the window with the Havana sunshine shining in on me, I smiled to myself as I imagined making an effigy of Alec Cartwright and sticking needles into it. Or better still, making an image of you and sticking needles into it. It was exactly what you deserved, and I imagined you jumping about with sudden mysterious pains as I put the needles into the effigy.

I was so absorbed in my reading and my pleasant fantasies, I would probably have missed Luis if he'd walked up to the café. However, Luis didn't walk. He drove up to the café. And not in some rusty old Russian car bearing the scars of numerous crashes either. No, of course not. Luis drove up in the most beautiful red Cadillac I'd seen since arriving in Havana. It had an open top and perfect paintwork, and Luis drove it with just one hand on the steering wheel. In the other hand he held a cigar, which he waved at me to say hello.

Everyone looked at him. The tourists, of course – half a dozen of them – surrounded his car to have their photographs taken almost as soon as he'd parked. But the ordinary Cubans looked too, at him and his car. Luis had such style, and he looked extremely good as he pushed open the doors of the café and walked towards me, a big smile on his face. I can't deny I felt a sense of pride that this was the man who'd held me in his arms in his bed that morning. The man who, hopefully, would be doing the same thing again later on.

'*Querida*,' he said in his deep voice, bending to kiss me on both cheeks. 'Tell me about your morning. What have you discovered so far about our Mr Mouthwash?'

'Enough to make him very miserable indeed,' I said, smiling up into his handsome face. 'Enough to blackmail his girlfriend and to destroy his dreams of happy-ever-after forever. Quite a victory for one morning, don't you think?'

Chapter 5 *Cadillac cruising*

Luis ordered coffee for himself and a refill for me, and then he sat and listened to my account of that morning's activities. He didn't seem as impressed as I'd expected him to be. In fact, by the time I'd finished, he wasn't looking very happy at all.

'What is it, Luis?' I asked him, puzzled. 'What's wrong?'

Luis stirred several spoonfuls of sugar into his coffee, then sighed, looking at me thoughtfully. 'I know that it is hard for you to imagine what it is like for Cubans,' he said. 'Cuba is our country, and we are proud to be Cuban. But at the same time we have no real hope for ourselves. No ambition. What is there to have ambition for? We are poor and we will be poor always. It is inevitable. A fact of our lives the way the sun coming up in the morning is a fact of our lives. Tourists, they come here to experience our country, but they leave without ever knowing what it is to be Cuban.'

'You don't want me to blackmail Gina, do you?' I guessed, and Luis shook his head.

'No, *querida*,' he said. 'You are right. I do not.' He sighed and took my hand in both of his. Then he looked deep into my eyes, willing me to understand. 'You see, it is probably true that Gina is . . . how do you say it? Exploiting. Yes, that is it. Gina is exploiting Alec Cartwright. Perhaps that is cruel, but I don't think so. Because he is exploiting her too, is he not? She is a victim too. No, the real cruelty in this case is to her man. To Carlos. And to Gina herself of course, because it is not right that she feels she has to be the pet of Alec Cartwright when all that she truly wants is to live with Carlos and to have many babies with him.'

By now, passion and strength of feeling had increased the volume of Luis's voice, and he was waving his hands in the air to emphasise his point. 'Do you think that Gina is happy lying in that old man's arms?' he asked. 'Do you think she smiles with affection as she lies in his bed and listens to him using his mouthwash? No, she does not! But I tell you, her mother will be happy about it.' He nodded when I looked doubtful. 'It is true, *querida*. Yes, I can assure you of this. Gina's mother will be delighted that her daughter has the chance to have money and a good life. The chance to escape.'

Luis shook his head at the injustice of it, then looked at me appealingly. 'No, Carla,' he urged me, 'do not blackmail Gina. Save her instead. Remove the man who stands in the way of her happiness with Carlos. Remove Alec Cartwright from her life.'

Remove Alec Cartwright from her life . . . Was that the moment, I wonder? The moment when my thoughts of revenge turned into thoughts of murder? I don't know. I wasn't aware of it at the time but, looking back, I realise now that there was a finality about the way Luis spoke that word: remove.

'All right,' I told him. 'I won't blackmail Gina. I didn't really want to anyway. She looks like a nice person.'

'She is a nice person,' Luis declared with authority, and I looked at him, surprised.

'Do you know her personally, then?' I asked, and he smiled.

'Of course,' he said. 'I know many, many people in Havana. And later today I will take you to meet Gina. We will have a little conversation with her about Alec Cartwright. But before that, finish your coffee. We will go for a drive.' He paused, looking at me. 'That is,' he asked, 'if you wish it?'

I glanced out of the window at the beautiful red car and then I turned back to grin at him. 'Yes please,' I said, and Luis laughed.

'Come on then,' he said, standing up. 'Let's go!'

The Cadillac was superb. So were the views. And so was Luis's company. I hadn't had so much fun for ages. I honestly don't think I thought about you once for two whole hours. Luis and I laughed together the whole time, and we waved and called out to people when they stopped to admire the car. And whenever we had to stop at traffic lights, we kissed. It was impossible to believe that I had known Luis for less than twenty-four hours.

But then something happened to remind me that I didn't really know him at all. He stopped the car by the Malecón sea wall and got out, glancing at me only briefly. 'Wait here for me please, *querida*,' he said. 'I have a little business to attend to.'

So I sat obediently in the Cadillac and watched Luis as he approached a group of men sitting on the wall. I wasn't close enough to see their expressions, but I was close enough to get the impression that they respected Luis. No, perhaps it was even more than that. Perhaps it was more that he dominated them. They smiled at him, and he shook hands with all of them, but somehow he seemed to be more powerful than any of them – almost as if he was their boss or something. Then, as I watched, I saw two of the men give him something, though I couldn't see what it was. If I had to guess, I'd say that it was money changing hands. Why, I didn't know. And perhaps I didn't want to know. Perhaps I suspected that Luis's business with the men was something illegal.

But anyway, when Luis returned, even though his smile was the same as ever, things seemed different between us somehow. He was the same Luis, and yet he was changed for me, perhaps because I now suspected he was some kind of criminal.

He seemed to guess something of what I was thinking, but he didn't offer me any explanations. Instead, he just smiled that charming smile of his and patted my knee. 'Come,' he said. 'Let us find Gina and have our conversation with her.'

I nodded. 'Yes,' I said, 'let's.' It was time to remember my reason for being in Havana. Time to get down to business.

Luis drove back into Habana Vieja, and I soon recognised the dark street where Gina had gone to meet Carlos. We didn't need to knock on the door however, because as soon as the Cadillac pulled up outside the house, both Carlos and Gina looked down into the street from the rusty balcony.

'Luis!' Carlos called down, and I smiled at Luis for probably the first time since leaving the Malecón sea wall.

'Is there anyone you don't know in Havana?' I asked him, and he grinned at me.

'There are still one or two people who are strangers to me,' he said, and then he directed his attention to the rusty balcony, speaking quickly in Spanish. There was no hope of me understanding, but it wasn't important. What was important was that five minutes later Gina was at ground level, kissing Carlos goodbye. Then, she climbed into the back of the car and we drove away.

'I have to start work at the hospital in one hour,' she said in Spanish, and I looked at her reflection curiously in the mirror, trying to decide whether she was anxious or not. But her pretty features were expressionless, and I decided that either she had no idea as yet who I was and what this was about, or that she was simply resigned to her fate.

Luis stopped the car a few blocks away and looked at me. 'OK,' he said, 'you have half an hour to convince her that she is making a mistake. You can speak in English. She will understand if you keep it simple. I will stand over there in case you need me to translate.' And with that, he got out of the car and leant against a wall to smoke a cigar.

I got out of the car myself and climbed into the back with Gina. She moved over a little to give me space, staring down at her hands to avoid looking at me.

'Gina,' I asked, 'do you know who I am?'

She looked up and spoke clearly. 'Yes, I know,' she said, meeting my eyes. 'You are the friend of Alec's ex-wife.'

I shook my head. 'No,' I said slowly, 'I'm not. I'm the friend of his wife. Alec isn't divorced, Gina. He's still married.'

Chapter 6   *Delivery girl*

I could tell it was a shock for Gina to discover that Alec was still married. And maybe it was cruel of me, but I'm afraid I didn't give her the chance to recover before I continued.

'Alec is married to a woman who really loves him,' I told her. 'They have three children – three daughters – and Alec's very close to them. Very close. He would never do anything to hurt them. He loves his wife too, I know he does. He isn't going to leave her.'

Gina wasn't looking at me. She was pulling at the material of her uniform with the fingers of one hand, her beautiful face looking miserable.

I sighed. 'Look, I know Alec's probably made you lots of promises, Gina,' I went on, 'but, according to Diane, you're not the first girl he's lied to like this. He does it all the time. I think he just loves the excitement of being with someone new. Especially someone young and pretty like you. But it never lasts. He always ends up going back to Diane, because deep down, he really loves and needs her.'

'In any case,' I told her, 'even if you do eventually manage to marry Alec, he'll soon get tired of you. That's what Englishmen are like. They only stay with a woman for a few years, and then they look for somebody else. And when that happens, you'll be trapped on your own in a cold wet country with no friends or family and no money to come back home to Cuba. You'll die a lonely old lady, dreaming about Carlos as you shiver by the fire.'

There were tears in Gina's eyes, but I couldn't really feel guilty because there was more than an element of truth in what I had told her. Besides, I did my best to make it up to her. As she sat there weeping at the very unattractive prospect I'd described, I reached into my pocket for the money I'd withdrawn from the bank earlier that day. Five hundred dollars. A lot of money for a girl like Gina. 'Here,' I said, holding it out to her. 'Take this; it's for you and Carlos. I know my friend would want you to have it. Forget all about Alec Cartwright and marry Carlos. You deserve a better life than the life Alec's offering you, Gina. You deserve to be happy.' I meant it; she did deserve to be happy.

Slowly she nodded and wiped her face with the back of her hands. Then she reached out and took the money, putting it away carefully in the front pocket of her dress. 'OK,' she promised at last, 'I will never see Alec again. It is finished.'

I tell you, I could hardly believe how easy it had been to convince her. I was relieved though, and very, very pleased. And when Luis stepped forward to suggest that Gina write a quick note to Alec telling him it was over, I agreed enthusiastically, imagining how fantastic it would feel to give the letter to him. When I watched Alec reading Gina's words and saw the heartbreak in his face, I would have done my duty towards Diane. My revenge, as far as Alec Cartwright was concerned, would be complete.

Or at least that's what I thought then.

We drove Gina to the hospital, and as I watched her

going in through the main entrance, I wondered – just for a moment – what she was thinking and feeling, now she knew she was likely to stay in Cuba for the rest of her life. I was only human after all, and I did have some sympathy for her situation.

'You have done her a favour, *querida*,' Luis assured me, turning the Cadillac around and setting off in the direction of his apartment. 'And now, you must do me a favour too.'

I looked at him quickly, and something in my expression made him laugh. 'Do not worry, *querida*,' he said. 'I only ask that you present the letter to Alec Cartwright as soon as possible so that he hurries back to England with his mouthwash at the earliest opportunity!'

I expect the relief showed in my face, because Luis laughed again. 'Did you think I was going to ask you to murder someone for me, my Carla?' he joked, his eyes sparkling, and when I laughed too, the rest of the tension between us disappeared.

'I think you're a man who's full of surprises,' I told him, and this belief proved true almost as soon as we got back to the apartment, when Luis took me to see his garden at the back of the apartment building.

'Luis, it's beautiful!' I said, admiring the flower borders and the pots. The garden was small but very attractive, with an area for tools and garden equipment and two comfortable garden seats as well as all the flowers. 'Did you do it all yourself?'

'But of course,' Luis said. 'Gardening is very relaxing for me. Yes, out here I have only the weeds to fight. And I have a good friend to help me to do that.' He smiled, pointing in the direction of a small, innocent-looking bottle standing among the gardening equipment. 'My weedkiller. It is very strong. Those weeds, they have not got a chance.'

I bent to smell some particularly beautiful red flowers. 'But,' I said, 'apart from battles with the weeds, it's peaceful out here.'

'Yes,' he agreed, 'mostly. Unless a certain person chooses to use his bathroom while I am tending my flowers.' He nodded in the direction of the low wall that separated his garden from its neighbour, then looked at me and smiled. 'However, let us not think of such unpleasant subjects. Please, sit in my garden and enjoy the flowers while I cook some dinner for us.'

I thanked him, taking him up on his invitation, and it wasn't long before the smell of cooking, combined with the scents and bright colours of his flowers, infected my senses until I felt almost drunk on it all. Cuba, I decided happily, was a very surprising, rich and exciting mixture. As unique and precious as a rare perfume.

All around me, in other gardens and on balconies, families were catching up on the events of their day, and I listened to their musical Spanish voices, closing my eyes to drink in every last drop of atmosphere.

Until suddenly, completely without warning, that atmosphere was brutally destroyed. Somebody, somebody very close by indeed, began to cough in a particularly unpleasant way; a really heavy, thick cough. The cough of a smoker who thinks himself alone.

I knew the cough belonged to Alec Cartwright. It had to. Apart from the fact that it was very close by, it was the kind of unselfconscious cough a loud mouthwash user would possess. My body instantly grew stiff with tension, and I was no longer aware of the family conversations around me or Luis's singing. I was suddenly too hot, my clothes wet through with sweat, and I think I knew vaguely that I was afraid, very afraid, though I didn't analyse why at the time. Looking back now, I suppose it was because I was about to meet the man I'd been thinking about ever since I'd arrived in Cuba. My first target for revenge.

Suddenly the cough stopped, and I held my breath, listening. I wasn't sure whether Alec Cartwright was still in his bathroom or not. But then I was presented with clear evidence that he was. First, I heard the sound of a toilet and then, a second or so afterwards, a window opened. And finally that awful coughing started up again, even louder now with the window open, combining with my nervous stomach to make me feel sick.

I tell you, I hardly dared to breathe, sitting there in Luis's garden, knowing that the man I'd travelled thousands of kilometres to find was actually standing in his bathroom, only a few metres away from me. And the strangest thing of all was that he didn't even know I was there. Not only that, but he was totally unaware of my existence. And the role I was about to play in his life.

I felt powerful actually, I think, even though my legs were trembling. Alec Cartwright's fate was in my hands, and I took Gina's letter from my handbag and looked at it, imagining the effect it was going to have on him. Already in my mind, I could hear the sound of that cough being replaced by the sound of Alec Cartwright's grief.

'Carla? What is it, *querida*? What is wrong? You are so very pale.'

Luis had come outside without me noticing, and I saw

vaguely that he was holding two glasses of rum. I walked shakily over to him so that I could whisper into his ear. 'Your neighbour's returned,' I said against his skin. 'I'm going to pay him a visit.'

Luis's eyes burned down into mine. 'Be patient, *querida*,' he urged me. 'Very soon he will come out into his garden, and then we can both witness his reaction.'

I hesitated for just a second before nodding my agreement to this plan. There was a selfish part of me that wanted to keep the destruction of Alec Cartwright's happiness to myself, but Luis had helped me to get this far, so I wasn't in a position to refuse him this request.

So I waited, and just as Luis had predicted, a few minutes later my patience was rewarded by the sound of a door opening, and footsteps bringing that cough outside. And then, finally, I got my first close-up view of Alec Cartwright. Mr Mouthwash.

He looked smaller somehow, on his own, without the beautiful Gina in his arms and the important medical building behind him. He just seemed like an ordinary overweight, middle-aged man with an unattractive beard and a cough. Harmless really, and for a second or two I think I hesitated, perhaps doubting whether I should give him Gina's letter at all. But fortunately, Luis touched me with his elbow, bringing me back to my senses.

'Excuse me,' I said nervously over the wall, moving towards him, and Alec Cartwright immediately looked round, surprised to hear an English voice.

'Yes?' he said, and something about his voice removed those last stupid doubts from my mind. 'Yes' is a very small word, it's true, but even so, Alec Cartwright managed to say it in a way which reminded me that he was an unpleasant man. A very unpleasant man. A man who had treated my good friend Diane like dirt.

'I have something for you,' I said, handing the letter to him over the wall.

He took it without a word, certainly without thanking me, his face remaining expressionless as he tore the envelope open. And that's exactly the way his face remained as he read the letter. Expressionless. It also describes the sound of his voice when he spoke to Luis after he'd finished the letter. Expressionless.

'Women!' he said calmly, in a man-to-man kind of voice. 'They always make the mistake of thinking they can't be replaced when, in actual fact, the very reverse is the case.' He looked down at the letter again, speaking to it as if it were Gina. 'My dear,' he said, 'your departure is an inconvenience, I assure you, and not the tragedy you so fondly seem to imagine it is.' And then he laughed. And if I hadn't hated him before, believe me, I hated him at that moment, with the darkest, blackest hatred it is possible to feel.

'Yes,' he said, smiling at Luis over the wall, 'women, eh?' And then he folded the letter up, put it into his top pocket, and disappeared back inside.

'I think you should sit down, Carla.' It was only when Luis spoke to me, that I realised I was feeling dizzy. That I was shaking from head to foot with a combination of anger, hatred and disappointment. In fact, my feelings were so extreme, I was in severe danger of fainting. It was the blanket in the dappled shade all over again, you see. It was almost as if you were looking at me and saying those words again: 'I'm sorry, Carla. I'm so sorry. There's no easy way to say this, so I'll just come right out and say it. I . . . I've met somebody else.' My failure to make Alec Cartwright suffer was like being rejected all over again.

I felt a glass being pressed against my lips, and when I opened my mouth obediently, the strong taste of rum filled my mouth. I swallowed automatically, and the strong liquid travelled down my throat and into my stomach, returning a little colour to my face.

Luis's arms were around me and his kindness made me want to cry, but I refused to give in to tears. I wanted to hold on to my anger instead; perhaps somewhere deep inside, I knew I would need it to give me strength for what I had to do next.

Luis and I talked for a while; or rather Luis talked to me, I've no idea what about. I expect he tried to tell me that we'd be able to find another way to deal with Alec, I don't know. Anyway, I eventually managed to convince him I'd be OK on my own, so he went back indoors to finish cooking our meal, only coming out again briefly to let me know that he'd seen Alec go out.

'He was wearing a suit,' he told me. 'So perhaps he has gone to find himself a new girlfriend.'

I nodded, but actually I wasn't interested in why Alec had gone out; I was only interested in the fact that he had. And that this meant that his apartment was now empty.

And I hadn't heard him lock his back door.

Chapter 7 *My first murder*

I tell you, I climbed over that wall and opened that door in less time than it takes to blink, and as easily as if I'd committed burglaries each day of my life since the age of six.

Except that burglary was the very last thing on my mind at that moment.

Once inside the apartment I paused, all my senses alert, checking that I was indeed alone. It was quite dark in the room after the bright sunshine outside, dark and untidy. I could see half-hidden shapes of furniture and junk; shapes that seemed strange and frightening in the darkness. But I could also hear the faint but familiar sounds of Luis in his kitchen coming through the wall from next door: his deep singing voice and the sharp sound of a spoon making contact with the side of a saucepan. It reminded me that at any moment Luis might come out to check up on me, and that there was no time to waste.

So I crept quickly through the room and out into the hallway, turning left to where I knew the bathroom must be. Once in the bathroom with the light on, it didn't take me long to spot Alec Cartwright's bottle of mouthwash. There it was, standing in pride of place in the centre of the shelf above his sink.

I don't think anyone can ever be truly aware of how they'll behave in such circumstances. Of what they're really capable of when they've been driven so very far. Quite beyond the point of compromise.

Am I trying to justify what I did next? Perhaps. I don't know. I only know that I was on the slippery slope heading towards becoming a murderer and, for whatever reason, I just didn't choose to stop myself from falling. It's as simple as that.

As I reached out and took that bottle of mouthwash down from the shelf and unscrewed the top, there were tears running down my face. But I wasn't crying because I was imagining Alec Cartwright dying a painful death in a few hours' time. No, not at all. As I took the top off the bottle of weedkiller I'd borrowed from Luis's garden and began to pour it into the bottle of mouthwash, I was imagining *your* face, not Alec Cartwright's. I was seeing you in the garden in the dappled shade. I was hearing your voice as you spoke the words that broke my heart into little pieces: 'I've met somebody else . . . I've met somebody else . . .'

As I said at the beginning, you're the murderer, not me.

Standing there at the sink in Alec Cartwright's bathroom, I took a few deep breaths to drive away the emotion. Emotion was a luxury I couldn't afford at that moment; I needed my brain to be perfectly clear if I wasn't going to give the game away or leave any evidence. So I took those deep breaths and then I carefully shook the bottle of mouthwash to mix the two liquids together. Once I'd finished, I held the bottle up to the light to check whether it looked OK. Fortunately, the weedkiller was colourless and the mouthwash was blue, so there were absolutely no signs of what I'd done. Wiping the bottle carefully with one of Alec Cartwright's towels, I replaced it on the shelf. Then I left the bathroom and went back the way I'd come, stopping only to wipe anything I remembered touching.

My eyes were used to the darkness now, and when I was nearly at the outside door, I paused, catching sight of a letter on the coffee table. Gina's letter. I picked it up and put it into my pocket with the weedkiller. Then I let myself out of the flat. Once outside, I climbed back over the wall and sat down in my chair in Luis's garden. The whole trip next door had probably taken me two minutes at the very most, but I was exhausted, and I had to just sit in that chair for several minutes, breathing as deeply as I could until my heart stopped beating so quickly.

Why did I pick up the letter? I can explain it now, looking back – I didn't want Gina to be connected to murder because I liked her. At the time I didn't think much at all; I just acted. It was as if a different part of my mind had taken over. A cold logical part of my mind that dealt with hiding evidence and coping with murder.

'Dinner is served, *señorita*,' Luis said brightly a few minutes later. He came out to fetch me with absolutely no idea of what I'd just done. I'm sure it was a very, very long time since Luis could accurately have been described as innocent, but he was definitely innocent at that moment, poor man. He wanted to impress me with his talents as a chef, I suppose, and that's what he was thinking about. It didn't occur to him to think that I'd just popped round to poison his neighbour's mouthwash while he was preparing dinner.

I managed to do justice to his cooking somehow, though

I shall never know how, because I had no appetite whatsoever. Pictures formed in my mind, very clear pictures of Alec Cartwright using his poisoned mouthwash. Trying to spit it out. Holding his throat and struggling to breathe. Collapsing onto the bathroom floor. Moving around on the floor like a fish taken out of the water. And finally lying there, dead, his eyes wide open and staring . . .

And all the time these pictures were in my mind, Luis and I ate our meal, drank wine and listened to music. We even laughed and joked, although I've no idea what about now. I didn't feel as if I was inside my body at all. It was almost as if I was floating in the air somewhere above the table, looking down at me and Luis talking and laughing below. Nothing seemed real at that table. The only reality was the bottle of mouthwash on the bathroom shelf next door, waiting for Alec Cartwright and his night-time habits.

'Do you have to work tonight?' I asked Luis after the meal was finally over. 'I'd love to go out dancing somewhere. Will you take me dancing, Luis? Please?' I looked at him appealingly as I spoke, moving my chair so that I could put my arms around his neck.

'I don't have to work until much later,' he said. 'We can go dancing before that. Yes, I would like to take you dancing. I will teach you to salsa!'

'Actually,' I told him, 'I can already salsa!'

But Luis didn't look convinced. 'Nobody can say they can dance the salsa until they have danced it in Cuba!' he said. I didn't bother to argue, partly because I suspected he was right, but mostly because I was anxious to go out before Alec Cartwright got back.

I really had fun with Luis that night. Yes, even though I knew that while we were dancing, Alec was probably dying on his bathroom floor. Luis was such a dynamic man, and he was also a superb dancer, expertly sweeping me along and spinning me around the dance floor. We'd stopped off at my hotel room so that I could get changed, and I'd chosen a dress with a full skirt. It flowed out around us as we danced, and I think we looked good together. We seemed to attract quite a lot of attention, anyway.

I smiled and I laughed and I pressed my face close to Luis's face whenever I could, and I didn't think about the bottle of weedkiller I'd placed in the hotel dustbin. Or Gina's letter, which I had torn into tiny pieces and got rid of down the toilet in the bar downstairs.

When Luis dropped me off at my hotel before he went off to his work, it was almost one o'clock in the morning and I was pretty sure that Alec Cartwright was already dead.

'You are sure that you do not want to wait for me at my apartment?' Luis asked me, holding me close to him outside the hotel entrance.

I reached up to kiss him. 'No,' I said. 'Come to me here. Room 217. Ask Reception to phone through to me and I'll unlock the door for you.'

'But you will be asleep,' he said, concerned, and I smiled.

'You're worth waking up for,' I told him, and he laughed.

'OK, see you later,' he said, giving me a final kiss before he left.

I watched him go, then I went into the hotel to tell the

receptionist to expect him. I wanted her to be able to confirm that she'd seen him if anyone asked her about it afterwards. I didn't want anyone to be able to accuse Luis of being in the flat next door when Alec Cartwright used his mouthwash.

What I didn't anticipate was that Luis would hear about the result of my plans so quickly. That he would come so silently into my hotel room when I opened the door to him, sit on the edge of my bed and wait for me to join him.

'Luis?' I hadn't put the light on when I answered the door, and I spoke his name uncertainly in the darkness.

When I heard him sigh, there didn't seem to be much point asking him what was wrong. Or in trying to deny it. 'Are you angry with me?' I asked him instead, my throat dry with tension.

'Angry?' he repeated slowly. 'I am not sure about that. In a strange way I suppose I admire you, although the drama of what you have done is a little . . . inconvenient, shall we say? A man like Alec Cartwright is easily lost in Havana if somebody wishes it, you understand. However, I appreciate that such a death is not as satisfying as the agony of a death from poison.'

'Have you been back to your apartment?' I asked him urgently.

'No,' he said, 'I have not. A friend came to find me. He warned me that an ambulance had taken my neighbour away to hospital, and that the police were asking questions.'

'He isn't dead?' I asked, covering my mouth with my hands in horror.

'Even the weeds do not die within minutes, *querida*,' Luis said, and his voice had grown very quiet suddenly. As quiet and as soft as silk. Dangerous.

'But . . .' I licked my lips nervously. 'He *will* die. Won't he?'

Luis nodded. 'Oh yes,' he said, still in that dangerously quiet voice. 'He will die. It will take several days, but yes, he will die. There is no cure for the effects of that poison.'

There was something about the sound of his voice that made me suddenly wonder whether I'd made a mistake when I'd decided to trust him. What if he blackmailed me? Or made me confess? What, after all, did I really know about him? He was involved in something illegal, I was sure of that. Unless his illegal activities were just a cover for the fact that he actually worked for the Cuban government . . .

My thoughts were beginning to spin out of control when Luis moved towards me on the bed.

'Where is the bottle of weedkiller, *querida*?' he asked, and suddenly I imagined myself locked away in a Cuban prison for the rest of my life. Or worse than that. Dead.

'Oh, it's safe,' I said. 'Honestly it is. That is . . . I mean, I got rid of it.'

Luis nodded, then reached across me to switch the bedside lamp on.

'Why don't you tell me all about it?' he suggested. 'Tell me everything.'

So I started to talk, my voice trembling, and all the time Luis stared deeply into my eyes. Sometimes he nodded, and sometimes he interrupted me to ask a question. And after I'd finished, there was silence for a moment. I honestly couldn't predict what he was going to do next. So,

I can tell you, I was very surprised indeed when what he *did* do was reach out and take me into his arms. And even more surprised when he kissed me . . . I responded to that kiss, of course, even though my mind was still going round and round like a washing machine on the spin programme. But I was still afraid.

It was a relief when Luis pulled away slightly. 'Do not worry, my Carla,' he said, and something in his face gave me a little bit of hope. 'Everything will be all right. I will see to it.'

It was exactly what I wanted to hear, and, as if by magic, my fear suddenly vanished. I laughed out loud with pure relief, and Luis laughed too, his laugh sounding deep and loud and comforting in the plain hotel room.

We started to kiss again after that, and, well, we made love too, of course. And yes, it was good. Very, very good. How could it be otherwise? Luis was a sophisticated, experienced man. Besides, our hearts and our minds were connected by a shared knowledge of murder.

Remember how we always used to fall asleep in each other's arms after we'd made love? Well, that's exactly what Luis and I did that night, and somehow I felt safer than I'd felt for a very long time. I trusted Luis, you see. We had something in common, he and I: we'd both been forced into being bad by our circumstances. And I knew Luis would do everything in his power to protect me.

So it was very disappointing to wake up the next morning and find myself alone.

There was a note from Luis on the pillow next to me. 'I suggest you leave Cuba as soon as possible, *querida*,' he had written. 'Change your flight and go today if you can. I will not mention you to the police, but anyway do not worry. What connection could you have to what has happened? Goodbye. I shall always remember you. Luis.'

But I couldn't take Luis's advice straight away because all the flights to Heathrow were booked up. It was almost three days before I managed to make my escape. I spent that time hidden in my hotel room, expecting the police to knock on my door at any moment. But nobody came; well, apart from Room Service that is, bringing food I didn't really want to eat. Not the police, not Luis, nobody. I watched television constantly, but there was no mention of the unexplained death of a foreigner.

Then, finally, on Wednesday morning, I settled my bill and left the hotel in a taxi. I boarded a plane for London Heathrow, and my adventures in Cuba were over.

However, my adventures in Norfolk, England were just about to begin.

Chapter 8 *A widow's grief*

I'd been away from England for less than a week, but even so, autumn seemed to have arrived while I'd been in Cuba.

The people in the train from London were all wearing jeans and jumpers, while I shivered in my shorts and T-shirt. Rain was falling against the train window, and the passing fields looked grey and empty. It was still just too early for the leaves to start changing colour, but the trees had a definite defeated look about them, as if they knew winter was already on its way.

All in all, it was a very depressing welcome home, as I'm sure you can imagine. My brain struggled to cope with the contrast between that view out of the train window and memories of events in Cuba. And, you know, for once I actually didn't think about you, but about Luis. Poor Luis, left behind in the exciting but hopeless environment that was Cuba. Forever.

And yet, somehow, it was impossible to imagine Luis anywhere else but Cuba. Certainly not here in England. What job could he do in England that would earn him enough money to support the kind of lifestyle he would surely want here? A job that allowed him to use all his charm and his intelligence, but which only required him to work a few hours each day?

No, Cuba was the right place for Luis to be and, whether I liked it or not, England was the right place for me to be. It just didn't feel like that on that depressing train journey back to Norwich, with the memories of Cuban sunshine fresh in my mind.

I had cheered up a bit by the time I got home though. For one thing, the sun had come out, and my little house always looks at its best when it's full of sunlight. There was a nice pile of letters waiting for me on the doormat too, and you know how I love to get post. And the red light on my answerphone was flashing. Call me childish if you like, but it felt good to know people had been thinking about me while I'd been away.

Anyway, I kicked off my shoes, pressed the 'play' button on the answerphone and sank into the comfort of my sofa to read my letters. I was halfway through a postcard from my brother, who was on holiday somewhere in Wales, when Diane's voice – sounding shaken and panicked – filled the room.

'Carla, I've got to talk to you. He's dead. Alec's dead. I had a phone call early this morning, and I can't believe it. I simply can't believe it. The girls are just . . . Well, their hearts are broken of course, and I . . . well, I don't know what to think, Carla. Look, please. Please phone me just as soon as you get back. I've got to know whether you saw him or not. Whether he said anything to you or — '

You'd hate my answerphone. It's the sort that gives people a time limit to leave their message, so it would be useless for most of your friends. Anyway, on this occasion it was useless for Diane because her time ran out and the machine made an ugly sound before it cut her off.

I was still looking at the photograph of the Welsh mountains on the front of the postcard. Or rather, my eyes were turned in that direction, but I couldn't focus on it properly.

Diane's voice still filled my head, and I felt confused and anxious. She'd sounded absolutely desperate; desperate and lost. And desperate and lost were the exact opposite of how I'd been expecting her to feel about the death of the dreadful Alec Cartwright. I'd been prepared for surprise, of course; but as she'd always spoken about him with such dislike and bitterness and I knew how badly he'd treated her, I suppose I'd expected her reaction to be one of relief.

As I sat there thinking about it, the phone rang again. When I answered, it was Diane herself.

'Good,' she said briefly. 'You're back. I'm coming round.'

'Diane, I —' I started to say, but it was too late. She'd already hung up. And fifteen minutes later she was on my doorstep, hammering on the door.

The minute I answered it, she burst inside, and I have to say she looked a mess. As I told you before, Diane usually looks fantastic, but that day, her hair wasn't even brushed, and she wasn't wearing any make-up. And worst of all, when she took her sunglasses off, I could see that her eyes were red and swollen from crying.

'Well?' she asked. 'Did you see him? Do you know anything?'

And right there and then, I decided to lie. Well, can you blame me? She was obviously really upset, and I . . . well, I just lost my courage.

I shook my head, and put a sympathetic arm around her shoulders. 'No, Di,' I lied softly. 'I did find out where he lived, but he wasn't in when I called round. And then when I tried again, it was already too late. One of the neighbours said he . . . Well, they told me he'd died. Oh, Di, I'm so very sorry.'

She totally believed me; that's the sad thing. Or anyway, judging by the way she broke down and cried as if her heart was broken, I'd say she believed me.

It was a very long time before she could speak, and then it went something like this. 'Who would do such a dreadful thing to him? He wasn't perfect, but he didn't deserve to die like that. Nobody deserves to die like that. Now there'll never be a chance for us to get back together again. Thank goodness I have you and my other friends; I don't know how I'd survive this otherwise . . .' etc.

Eventually she was exhausted, and I drove her home in her car. Her daughters arrived just as I was leaving, and I could tell they'd been crying as well. Diane collapsed into their arms, and all four of them burst into an explosion of tears right there in the hall.

I made my escape at that point, but none of them even noticed me leave, and I walked back home again feeling completely puzzled. Their grief was a mystery to me. But then, I'd seen Alec kissing Gina passionately in front of the medical building. And only a short while after that I'd witnessed him opening that rejection letter from her in his garden. Seen the expression on his face and the coldness in his eyes.

'Women!' he'd said. 'They always make the mistake of thinking they can't be replaced when, in actual fact, the very reverse is the case.'

'He didn't care about you!' I wanted to run back and shout at the four crying women. 'The only person Alec Cartwright cared about was himself!' But of course I didn't go back and I didn't say any such thing. They wouldn't have believed me anyway.

I did feel a little lonely walking back to my house from Diane's though. I suppose it had suddenly hit me that the only person in the entire world who knew what I'd done was Luis. And he was thousands of kilometres away in Cuba. I could never tell anybody else about it because of the risk of being arrested. It had to remain my personal secret forever.

And yet, I couldn't regret what I'd done. Alec Cartwright had deserved to die; I knew that. And some time in the future, Diane and her daughters would come to realise that too. And then they would be grateful to his murderer.

Chapter 9 *A cheap disguise*

I started planning my next murder straight away. Well, I suppose that's not strictly true. I *did* make plans to seek out Terry, Gemma's ex-husband, but at that stage I again only had thoughts of revenge in my mind. I'd managed to convince myself that the Alec Cartwright affair had been a one-off, the result of unique circumstances.

Anyway, the day after I got back from Cuba, Gemma and I met for coffee in Norwich city centre in a café overlooking the market place. Gemma reminds me of your sister (except Gemma's far more beautiful). She loves talking, Gemma does, just like your sister, and we sat there in the café and she chatted on about her family and Diane and the mystery of what had happened in Cuba. I made the occasional contribution to the conversation, but Gemma never needs much encouragement to speak, and most of the time I was free to daydream.

So I drifted in and out of the conversation, my mind absorbed in the view of the busy market place and the severe architecture of City Hall, the council building, standing behind it on the hill. I suppose a part of me was still in Cuba, and it was probably inevitable that I would make comparisons between Norwich and Havana. Norwich Market was practically bursting with the latest fashions and fresh fruit and vegetables, and the contrast between this and the aching poverty of similar markets I'd seen in Havana was huge.

'I had an awful argument on the phone with Terry the other day,' Gemma said at last, regaining my full attention.

'Why?' I asked. 'What's he done now?'

'Well,' Gemma said, her pretty face suddenly marked by frown lines. 'You know my daughter Kirsty is getting married next month? Well, Terry's insisting on bringing Sharon, his latest woman, to the wedding. He says he won't come otherwise, and you know how upset Kirsty will be if he doesn't turn up. But honestly, Carla, you should see this Sharon; she's *awful*. So cheap-looking. She'll turn up to the wedding wearing a low-cut top and short skirt, I just know she will. I don't want her there, spoiling things, I really don't. I haven't mentioned anything to Kirsty about it yet of course, but I tell you, Carla, I don't know what to do about the situation, I honestly don't.'

It occurred to me suddenly that Gemma sounded a bit like a child. A spoilt child who hasn't got exactly what she wanted for her birthday. Perhaps she wasn't quite as nice as I'd first thought. But then the truth was I didn't really know her very well. I didn't know any of my new friends very well.

Anyway, my new opinion of Gemma wasn't enough to put me off. You see, I never forgot that by taking revenge for my friends, I was actually practising taking my revenge on you.

'Where did you say Terry lives?' I asked casually.

'He still lives at Forest Grange, our family home,' she answered, sounding bitter about the fact. 'It's out in the countryside, just the other side of Wroxham. Why do you ask?'

'No reason,' I lied. 'I just wondered. Does she live there too? This Sharon?'

Gemma shook her head. 'No, she lives in Norwich somewhere. Although from what I can gather, she stays with Terry most of the time. Did I tell you he's having a swimming pool built? That must be for *her* to sunbathe beside, because the Terry I lived with for all those years couldn't even swim.' She sighed. 'I don't know, Carla,' she said, 'life's so unfair, isn't it? Since I left Terry, his business has been doing so well it practically manages itself these days.'

'What is his business?'

'He runs a riding stables. Only, I get the impression he hardly goes into work at all any more. Unless he fancies a ride himself, that is. He's got a manager to do everything for him. He spends all his time riding his horses and watching his swimming pool being built. And, no doubt, making love to his awful girlfriend. Did I tell you she was almost the same age as Kirsty?'

We parted company shortly after that; Gemma to do a bit of clothes shopping to help her forget about Terry, and me to go home to catch up on some sleep.

Later, after I'd woken up and had a snack, I got the car out and drove to Wroxham. By then it was about six thirty and the rush-hour traffic was just coming to an end. I didn't know exactly where to look for Forest Grange, but I knew the general direction it was in, so I drove slowly up and down the lanes searching for it.

I was just about to turn the car around and go back to ask for directions at a pub I'd passed a few kilometres back when I spotted a big white house set back from the road behind some fir trees. I slowed down to look at the house name at the end of the driveway. Forest Grange. I'd found it.

I didn't turn into the drive, and neither did I find somewhere to park near the house to wait in case Terry passed. I knew I needed a more subtle approach than that. Instead, I drove back to Norwich, working out my plan of action as I went.

This time I wouldn't be able to count on my victim's neighbour to help me to achieve my revenge. Terry's nearest neighbour was the pub, the King's Arms. Unless . . . Just as I was driving over Wroxham Bridge, I remembered seeing a sign outside the King's Arms advertising bed and breakfast. Terry was likely to be a regular at the pub, and if I stayed there, I'd meet him sooner or later. And even if he didn't come in, the landlord would know about him. I could pretend to be a tourist wanting to learn how to ride.

But first of all I needed a disguise. Unlike Havana, Wroxham was only a few kilometres from Norwich. I needed to be completely anonymous. Besides, a disguise would be fun.

Do you remember that fancy dress party we went to a few years ago? When you went as Elvis Presley, and I dressed up as a pop star with a long blonde hairpiece and leather trousers? Well, that's the look I adopted for my disguise. Except that I wore a short red skirt and high heels instead of the leather trousers. My make-up was just as heavy though. I even managed to match my lipstick exactly with the skirt.

I tell you, by the time I'd put on a low-cut, tight-fitting black top, I looked exactly the way Gemma thought Sharon was going to look at Kirsty's wedding. When I looked at my reflection in the mirror, I hardly recognised myself. The long blonde hair on its own would have made me look completely different, but the long, blonde hair *and* the clothes together . . . Well, I honestly don't think you'd have recognised me if you'd walked past me in the street.

Anyway, I packed a change of clothes and a few essentials into an overnight bag, and jumped back into my car. And by eight o'clock that evening I was installed in the bar at the King's Arms with a rum and coke in front of me and my overnight bag in the best guest room upstairs.

The landlord was called Gordon, and he was very friendly. The pub wasn't busy, so he was leaning on the beer pumps with his shirt-sleeves rolled up, chatting to me. I'd told him my tourist and horse-riding story, and he'd given me a list of possible stables to try the next day, including Terry's.

'Forest Grange Riding Stables would be able to sort you out,' he assured me. 'They're definitely the nearest. I don't think they're too busy now either, with all the kids back at school for the new term. Madeleine might be in here later with her boyfriend. I'll introduce you if I get the chance.'

'Is she the owner?' I asked, and he shook his head.

'No, the manager. The owner lives near here too, but I don't think he'd be able to tell you if they could fit you in for lessons. No, Madeleine's the one you need.'

But in the end neither Madeleine nor Terry came into the pub that evening. I didn't feel as if all my efforts with the fancy dress had been wasted though. I'd had the chance to practise being the type of woman my clothes suggested I was, and I had proof that my disguise was a success. There was a crowd of men around me by the end of the evening, and I don't think they were there to listen to my intellectual conversation.

You men really are pathetic, you know. Why can't you see how false all that make-up and hair colour makes us women look? But then that's it, isn't it? You don't want reality, any of you. Reality is boring. Reality gives you itchy feet. That's because you're all so shallow.

Anyway, I fully exploited the shallowness of the male sex the next morning by putting on my low-cut black top again. Only this time, because of the prospect of riding, I wore it with trousers. Really *tight* trousers. And loads of make-up, of course. Downstairs, I ate a light breakfast while Gordon chatted on about a late-summer barbecue he was organising for his regulars the following Saturday. Then I said my goodbyes and headed out to my car. Turning out of the pub, I drove off in the direction of Forest Grange. This time, when I got there, I indicated left and turned into the drive. And when I got to the house, I stopped the car and got out.

Arranging my long hair attractively around my shoulders, I fixed a pleasant smile onto my painted lips and knocked firmly on the front door. After a bit of a wait, it was answered by a man – Terry, I guessed – wearing a white towelling dressing gown. His hair – what there was of it – was standing up on end, and he needed a shave. I'd obviously got him out of bed.

There was a short pause while he looked me up and

down, adjusting his annoyed expression to one of surprise and pleasure.

'Is this Forest Grange Riding Stables?' I asked him sweetly. 'Oh dear, I haven't made a mistake, have I? I have come to the right place, haven't I?'

Terry smiled at me, hastily smoothing down his hair and pulling the belt of his dressing gown tighter. 'Well,' he said in an attractively deep voice, 'this isn't the stables, but I wouldn't call waking up and finding *you* on my doorstep a mistake.'

'Terry,' called a female voice from somewhere indoors. 'Who is it? Come back to bed. I'm missing you already.'

Terry's only acknowledgement of the voice was to step out onto the doorstep, pulling the door almost closed after him. 'The stables are along the next turning on the right,' he told me. 'I'm going there for a ride later this morning myself, actually. I hope you'll still be there then. I'm the owner, you see; I could give you a guided tour if you like.' He held out his hand. 'Terry Montague.'

Automatically, I put my hand into his and he shook it firmly. 'Vienna Francis.' I introduced myself, giving him the name I'd used at the pub. (Yes, I know, *Vienna*! I can just imagine how amusing you'd find that. But I don't care what you think. *I* think it's got style.) 'That's a very generous offer,' I told him. 'Thank you, I'd like a tour very much.'

Terry's smile turned into a satisfied grin. 'Great! Well, run along and have your lesson, and I'll see you afterwards. If I'm not around, just ask for me. Bye for now.' He waved his fingers at me then went back inside, presumably to return to bed and the impatient Sharon, and I got back into my car and followed his directions to the stables.

As you know, I grew up in horse-riding country. I went riding every Saturday right through my teens. My dad resisted buying a horse despite extreme pressure from me, but the horse I rode every week – Lightning, he was called – almost felt like my very own; I knew him and his habits so well. Anyway, the point is, I don't need riding lessons. When you have that much experience at something, you don't forget how to do it overnight. And after I'd got to the stables and convinced Madeleine of that, I was allowed to go riding through the woods near the stables on my own.

It was really enjoyable actually. The weather had cheered up a little, and the sunlight was slicing through the trees, leaving pools of light on the ground. It was really pretty, and for the first time since returning from Cuba, I felt good about being back in England. I allowed myself to simply enjoy the ride, and didn't think at all about Terry. Or you, or Luis, or Alec Cartwright. In fact, it was only when I turned my horse around and headed back towards the stables that I started to think about the whole revenge thing again.

Judging by Terry's response to me on his doorstep, it seemed reasonable to conclude that it wasn't going to be too difficult to get him away from Sharon. Terry seemed like the kind of man who would cheat on his woman without a second thought.

Unfortunately, this probably meant that using blackmail for revenge wasn't a very promising option. Because, if Terry didn't really care about Sharon at all, then he wasn't likely to be bothered if Terry and I had a love affair and I threatened to tell her about it.

No, blackmail probably wouldn't work. Unless, of

course, I could discover some other scandal Terry wanted to keep quiet.

Knowing my best immediate plan was to get to know Terry better, I urged my horse on towards the riding stables to see whether he'd arrived yet.

I didn't see him at first. Madeleine took the horse from me and we exchanged a few words about my ride and the pleasantness of the woods. When I asked her whether Terry was around, she pointed me in the direction of a low stable block on the other side of the yard. I said goodbye to her and walked across to it.

As I got close, I heard a man shouting, and I slowed down to listen. It was Terry. 'Stand still, you disobedient beast you!' he was saying, and as I listened, I heard a distinct slapping sound and the frightened response of a horse. 'I said, stand still!' Terry shouted again, and this was followed by yet another slap.

I really hate cruelty to animals, as you well know. Remember the shock you got when we got the puppy and I thought he needed more attention than just one meal and one walk a day? You were jealous because I thought of him as more of a companion than a pet, refusing to leave him shut up in the house on his own. Well, the way I see it, animals trust us. They're defenceless, completely dependent upon us. And only cowards abuse them.

So you can imagine, I expect, how I felt standing outside those stables, listening to Terry abusing his horse. I was sick to my stomach, and so furious that I think, if I'd had a knife or some other weapon with me, I'd have rushed straight into that stable and used it on Terry without a single thought for the consequences.

But I didn't have a weapon, and somehow I forced myself to wait, to stand in that stable yard and take a series of deep breaths until I was a little calmer. But looking back now, I tend to think that Terry's fate was sealed right there and then, as I stood listening to that terrified horse. Blackmail certainly seemed far too good for him anyway, and I was suddenly convinced that the world would be a better place without him in it.

'Well, hello there!' Terry finally came out of the stable, smiling at me as if he had never been in a bad temper at all. Somehow, I don't know how, I managed to smile back at him as if nothing was wrong.

'Hello!' I said brightly. 'Isn't it a lovely day? I've just had the most delightful ride through the woods!'

'I am pleased about that,' he said, looking me up and down. 'And your timing is perfect. I was just going to make myself a cup of coffee. Why don't you join me, and then we can do that guided tour.'

I agreed to all this, and he took me to the office, talking cheerfully all the way about goodness knows what. And all the time – walking across the yard, inside the office and, later, on the tour of the stables – Terry was always standing just a little too close to me. It was a deliberate invasion of my space; I was breathing the same oxygen as Terry, experiencing an intense charm attack. My nostrils were filled by the smell of his aftershave, my ears with the soft deepness of his voice. He looked me directly in the eyes as he spoke, and at every opportunity he reached out to touch my leg.

I hated Terry because of how he had just treated his horse and of course how he had treated Gemma, and yet I was still extremely aware of his attractiveness. Because he *was* attractive. Oh, he was middle-aged with an over-large stomach and hair going a little thin on top, but he possessed the self-confidence of someone who's been attractive all his life. Someone who's used to having women falling at his feet.

Of course he had no doubt whatsoever that I was going to be his next victim, and obviously I did all I could to encourage this belief. I laughed a lot, and I touched *his* leg when I spoke. I looked deeply into his eyes and I did my best to give him the impression that he was the most entertaining and attractive man I'd ever had a conversation with in my entire life.

And, by the end of the guided tour, Terry had invited me to dinner that evening at his house.

'Eight o'clock,' he said. 'And make sure you're hungry. I'm an excellent cook.'

I smiled into his eyes. 'I'm sure you're very talented,' I said, deliberately licking my lips.

As Terry watched my tongue travel over my lips, he made a little sound of desire. I think he wanted to grab hold of me right there in the stable yard, actually. Anyway, it was obvious to me that it wasn't only going to be Terry's cooking on the menu that night.

'Until eight o'clock then,' he said, leaning towards me to kiss my cheek.

'Until eight,' I agreed, beginning to walk away. Then I hesitated, looking back at him over my shoulder. 'By the way,' I said, 'won't your girlfriend object to me coming to your house? Or is she going to be there too?'

He did a good job at looking surprised. 'Oh,' he said.

'Do you mean the woman who was there this morning? Oh, don't worry about her. That's just a very casual relationship, nothing important. I'll send her home to Norwich. We'll be completely alone, I promise you.'

'Good,' I said with a final smile, then turned and walked slowly away towards my car, making sure I moved my hips the way Gina had moved hers in the streets of Old Havana. Like a salsa dancer. A *sexy* salsa dancer.

Chapter 10 *Vienna in Hawaii*

By the time I got back to the King's Arms, I had a terrible headache. It had really taken a lot out of me to hide the way I felt about Terry, I can tell you. And it's absolutely exhausting pretending to be somebody else.

But I think the main reason my head hurt the way it did was because Terry's words were still beating around my brain. 'Do you mean the woman who was there this morning?' he'd said. 'Oh, don't worry about her. That's just a very casual relationship, nothing important.'

Is that what you said about me when you met her on that skiing holiday? Is it? 'Oh, don't worry about Carla; that's just a very casual relationship; nothing important.' I bet you did say that, or something very similar. And, you know, I loved you. I really loved you. Just as Sharon probably loved Terry. As Gemma had once loved him. And Diane had loved Alec Cartwright. Oh yes, it was hatred making my head ache all right. Pure hatred.

But I had a bit of a sleep and a nice long bath, and by the time I had my Vienna Francis disguise back on, I felt a lot better. I was wearing the short red skirt and high-heeled shoes again, and I felt more than reasonably confident that Terry would approve of both.

'Bye, Vienna!' Gordon called to me from behind the bar. 'Whoever he is, he's a very lucky man!'

As I waved goodbye to him and left the pub, I felt a shiver of excitement run down my spine. I had no idea what I was going to do in order to get revenge for Gemma, but that lack of knowledge was half the thrill.

Terry came to the door dressed in white trousers, a blue Hawaiian shirt with bright red flowers on it and sunglasses. His appearance was quite a surprise, I must say, and he laughed when he saw my expression.

'I thought we'd have a Hawaiian-style evening,' he explained. 'To celebrate my new swimming pool.' And he proceeded to place a large orange flower behind my ear.

I smiled at him, reaching up to touch the flower rather nervously and secretly wondering whether Terry was mad. But when he bent to kiss me I smelt his breath and realised that he had been drinking.

'We've got Hawaiian music, and I'm cooking Hawaiian-style chicken,' he said, taking my hand and leading me into the house. 'And there's a fruit punch. A very strong fruit punch, if you know what I mean! My own recipe. Would you like to try a glass now?'

'I'd love to.' I smiled.

'Right! Back in a minute!'

When Terry left to get me a drink, I looked around. The lounge was mainly white, with white leather sofas and square black coffee tables. There was also a red sheepskin rug in front of a huge fireplace, and lots of mirrors. The room was full of expensive fashionable furnishings but it didn't feel like a home. It didn't seem genuine somehow, but it did suit someone who dressed in loud shirts and who wore sunglasses indoors. And from what I could see, Sharon didn't seem to have made any impression on it. There was no evidence that she spent any time there at all.

'One extra strong fruit punch,' Terry said, returning.

I took the glass from him. 'Thank you,' I said, and tried some. The punch did taste of fruit, but only just; it tasted more of alcohol. Very strong alcohol. Clearly Terry wanted to get me very drunk, very quickly. 'Oh, it's nice, Terry,' I told him. 'Very nice.'

He smiled. 'It is, isn't it? And just wait until you try the chicken. It's my speciality, even if I do say so myself.'

'I'm sure it is,' I said, trying some more of my punch. 'And your house is so lovely too. You've got such excellent taste.'

'I like to think so,' he boasted. 'But you haven't seen anything yet. Come and see my new pool!' He took my free hand and was about to sweep me from the room when the phone started to ring.

'Damn!' he swore. 'I'd better answer that. You go on ahead. Down the hall to the end and through the glass doors. I won't be long.'

I started to follow his directions, but as soon as I was out of sight, I stopped and waited to see whether I could hear his telephone conversation. I could, easily. Whether it was because he was a bit drunk, or because he was angry, I don't know, but I could hear every word. And I very quickly realised who he was speaking to.

'Look, I don't want to talk about the wedding now. It's weeks away. No, I'm not being unreasonable; you're the one being unreasonable. Such ridiculous attention to detail! Anyone would think you were inviting the royal family. Yes, I know she's my daughter. I should know; I'm the one who's paid for her clothes and her cars and her horses all these years. Don't be ridiculous! Of course I love her! What has that got to do with anything?'

By that point, I'd heard enough. I'd already decided that Terry was an extremely unpleasant man, and I'd just had that opinion completely confirmed.

The swimming pool, when I got there, was the kind of pool you'd expect to find in the home of a Hollywood film star. Not the kind of pool belonging to somebody who felt he needed to complain about the cost of maintaining his only daughter. At least that isn't a fault I can accuse you of; you were never mean with money. And you were certainly never mean towards your daughters. They always got everything they wanted. Sometimes even before they knew they wanted it! To be frank, they were spoilt.

Anyway, I sat myself down at a table by the poolside to wait for Terry, listening to the Hawaiian music and wondering how to kill him. Because I knew, by then, that I was going to kill him. It was exactly what he deserved. I just didn't know how I was going to do it.

I looked around the poolside for a suitable weapon, but there was nothing immediately obvious. There were some large, heavy-looking vases which looked as if they could knock somebody out if you hit them over the head with one, but a giant vase is hardly a subtle weapon. Leaning against one wall, there was a large net on the end of a long pole, presumably for fishing leaves out of the pool, and next to it there was a display of tropical plants, but I doubted whether any of them were poisonous, and I had no way of finding out. There were some large stones arranged on the ground around the plants though, and I quickly picked one up and put it in my handbag, in case it came in useful later.

The last thing I did before Terry made an appearance

was to pour my punch into a plant pot. It was essential for me to keep a clear head so I had to remain sober. However, it would definitely help my plans if Terry got even drunker than he was now.

When Terry finally appeared he had a big smile on his face. He also had a jug of punch in one hand and a dish of food in the other. 'Starters,' he said, placing the dish on the table in front of me. 'Help yourself.'

You'd have been so surprised if you'd been able to see me at that poolside sharing that meal with Terry. I was very calm. And entertaining. I laughed at Terry's jokes as if they were the funniest jokes I'd heard in my life and pretended I was as drunk as he was. But every time Terry walked unsteadily into the house to fetch more punch or more food, I fed the contents of my glass to one of the plants.

There was no way Terry could have predicted how vulnerable he became as he drank more. And when he finally moved unsteadily towards me to try to take me into his arms, it only took a very little push to keep him away.

'No, Terry,' I said gently.

'Oh, yes!' he said, coming at me again, and this time I pushed him harder. Very hard. You know I've always enjoyed going to the gym. Well, my arm muscles are very strong these days. OK, I wouldn't have been able to push Terry into the pool if he'd been sober, but he wasn't sober. He was very drunk indeed.

There was a huge splash when his body hit the water. Huge. The water shot right up into the air and splashed down again like a waterfall. Terry had landed face down and was soon gasping for breath. But I didn't give him the chance to breathe properly. I reached for the net and put it into the water, pole end first. Not to try to save Terry. Oh, no. To push him under. Time and time again. Push, push, push. Until finally he sank beneath the surface and all I could see were bubbles.

And then the bubbles stopped, and I had committed my second murder.

Chapter 11 *Ice cream monsters*

I haven't written anything in this book for several months now. After the past few terrible months, I haven't had the heart for it. In fact, I was going to stop there, to leave my story incomplete. But in the end I decided to carry on with it. It stops me from going completely crazy, writing it all down. And it helps to fill the long empty hours.

It's all so very strange, looking back. Christmas is almost here now, and in some ways those events of early autumn seem so distant. Sometimes it's as if I'm looking back through a telescope, but I've got the telescope the wrong way round. I can see myself, and yet I'm just a tiny dot in the distance.

At other times it's as if the telescope's the right way round and I'm looking directly into my face. Everything's close up, and I can see all the changing emotions crossing my features. And that's when I know that the memories will always be preserved in my mind, just as fresh and as strong as if it all happened yesterday. A living nightmare.

I suppose I'd gained rather a false sense of security about killing after two relatively easy murders. I certainly wasn't anticipating any difficulties when I set out to meet Cathy's ex, a couple of weeks after Terry died.

But I haven't told you about that yet, have I? About what happened after I killed Terry. Well, to be honest, the answer is nothing; nothing happened. At least, not to me. Oh, a full-scale murder investigation took place, but nobody ever connected the mysterious Vienna Francis at the stables with me.

There was one very disappointing incident though. Actually, it was almost a repeat of what had happened with Diane after I'd returned from Cuba. The disappointment was Gemma, her reaction to Terry's death. I can still hear her voice when she phoned to tell me about it – full of self-pity and anger. She actually blamed Terry for spoiling their daughter's wedding by dying. How logical is that?

'He always was a selfish man!' she said. 'He could never do anything right. Getting himself murdered like that within weeks of his daughter's wedding! How can poor Kirsty get married with all this going on? The shame of it all. We'll have to cancel all the arrangements! The poor girl will have to go to a funeral instead!'

As I put the phone down, I began to think my friends were very ungrateful indeed. Of course, they didn't know they had anything to thank me for, but they could, at least, have been grateful to fate, if nothing else. The men who had made their lives a misery for so long had been removed. They were now both free to move forward. To grow. To find happiness. I'd done them both a big favour, and all they could do was moan about it.

Actually, do you know what it reminded me of? It reminded me of all those times I had dragged myself to the supermarket in search of something your daughters would eat. Then I'd return home, loaded down with heavy carrier bags and I'd spend another hour chopping, stirring and cooking. And were they grateful when I put those lovingly prepared meals down in front of them at the table? No, they were not. They said things like: 'What's this?' 'This is disgusting!' 'I don't want to eat this, Daddy!' The darling princesses.

Well, I felt there was more than a hint of princess behaviour in the way both Diane and Gemma had reacted to the death of their no-good husbands. So it was quite encouraging when Cathy phoned me to spill her heart out about the thoughtlessness of *her* ex.

Poor little Cathy, she's always been the most vulnerable of the four of us. Often suffering from depression and dependent upon the unwilling Pete for financial support, she hardly ever saw her little son.

'Pete says he can't afford to give me any money any more,' she cried down the phone to me. 'He says I should look for more work. And he knows I find the amount of work I already do completely exhausting. It's a struggle to survive as it is. How can he expect me to stop getting depressed when he's behaving like this?'

I offered Cathy a few words of comfort, asked just enough questions to find out roughly where Pete lived, and then set out almost immediately to carry out my plans for revenge. I was convinced that Cathy, at least, would be grateful to me. For one thing, although Cathy and Pete had been separated for over a year, they weren't divorced. So if Pete died, Cathy would inherit his money. And her son would go back to living with her all the time. It all seemed very simple and straightforward as I left my flat on that sunny September morning. I had no idea what was about to happen to me. Of how very complex my life was about to become.

Pete was an engineer when I met him, living on the edge of Norwich in a village called Trowse. Trowse is a small place, very pretty. There's a river, a couple of lakes, some woods, a bakery and a pub. Oh, and a boat club. Pete loved to sail. In Trowse, it's possible to imagine you're in the countryside when the city is only a kilometre or two away. Pete liked it because, as he said to me on that day we first met, 'I've got the best of both worlds here. The stars above my garden and a supermarket around the corner.'

Anyway, as I've said, Trowse is a small place and, although I didn't know the number of Pete's house that morning when I set out to find him, I did know it was on the road leading to the lakes at Whitlingham Country Park. I was familiar with Whitlingham because I'd gone for a walk there in the summer with Cathy, her son Ben and her little dog Chalkie. And now I came to think of it, I could remember little Ben pointing out of the car window and saying, 'There's Daddy's house! There's Daddy's house!'

Of course, after all this time, I couldn't remember which house it had been, so I parked in the car park at Whitlingham Country Park and walked back along the road, casually looking at each house in search of clues.

Well, I found a clue all right. More than a clue. Evidence, solid evidence. Ben. I walked around a corner and there he was, in the front garden of one of the cottages. And as soon as he saw me, he tore open the garden gate and threw himself into my arms.

'Carla!' he shouted. 'Carla! Carla! Carla!'

I hugged him automatically, and as I did so a shadow made me aware that he wasn't alone. I looked up, straight into the deep brown eyes of a man I knew must be Pete.

'Well,' he said, smiling, 'I think your name must be Carla.' And he laughed.

Ten minutes later, the three of us were sitting on a blanket in the front garden, eating ice creams from Pete's freezer. Little Ben was chatting away to me, describing a boat trip he and his father had gone on the previous day, and his strawberry ice cream was melting right down the front of his T-shirt. His hands were pink and so was his mouth. There were even pink spots on the blanket next to him.

'Do you think my son's turning into an ice cream?' Pete asked me, and Ben laughed with delight.

'Don't be silly, Daddy!' he said.

'Or perhaps,' said Pete, 'he's turning into an ice cream *monster . . .*'

Ben approved of this idea, and he leapt up, holding his ice cream out in front of him like a weapon. 'Yes, Daddy, I'm an ice cream monster!' he cried excitedly, and for the next few minutes he proceeded to chase his father around the garden.

As I watched them, it was impossible not to smile at the fun they were having. They looked so alike, with their curly brown hair and dark eyes. I never had been able to identify any of Cathy's features or characteristics in little Ben, and now I knew why. He took after his father.

I expect you can already see the picture I'm beginning to paint for you. A pretty cottage, flowers in the garden, hardly any traffic to disturb the peace. Sunshine, strawberry ice cream and the sound of male laughter. Father and son. A contented unit, like you and the girls were whenever I wasn't around.

You never thought I was very good with children, did you? It never occurred to you to consider whether the three of you made it easy for me to fit in, to become a true part of your happy unit. You made your decisions and you consulted me afterwards. Or rather, you made your decisions and then just announced them to me. Come to think of it, there was very little consultation involved at all.

That day in Pete's garden, I felt included straight away. When they were both worn out from their ice cream monster game, father and son collapsed next to me on the blanket, laughing and struggling to get their breath. Ben took my hand, examining my arm carefully. 'You're very brown, Carla,' he said. 'Have you been on holiday?'

'I have. To Cuba,' I told him.

'Where's Cuba?' Ben wanted to know. 'Is it further away than London?'

Pete laughed, but I nodded seriously. 'Yes, it's much further away than London,' I told him. 'It's very far away. Across the sea, near America.'

'I'm going to go to Cuba one day!' Ben announced, and then he got bored sitting on the blanket and ran off to chase a butterfly which was flying above the flowers.

When we were alone, Pete leant on one elbow to look at me. 'Ben obviously likes you a lot,' he said. 'Have you spent much time with him?'

'I've only met him three or four times,' I said, thinking about it. 'But I like him a lot too. He's a lovely little boy.'

Pete smiled, watching his son. 'Yes, he is,' he agreed. 'Which is something of a small miracle, considering some of the things that have happened during his short lifetime. Though, actually, I think Cathy's periods of illness have probably made the two of us closer. We were together a lot while she was in hospital or resting.'

'Did she go to hospital?' I asked. 'I didn't know that.'

'Oh yes,' he said, 'four times altogether during our marriage. She's also tried to kill herself twice.' He looked at me. 'You didn't know that either, did you?'

I shook my head. 'No,' I said, 'I didn't.'

He frowned, then shook his head. 'I'm sorry,' he apologised. 'This is an unpleasant subject for a very pleasant afternoon.' He made himself smile. 'You didn't say what you were doing in Trowse.'

'Oh,' I replied casually, 'just exploring. I haven't lived in the area for that long.'

'Oh?' he said. 'And what made you move here?'

I gave a him a bitter little smile. 'Let's just say it's another unpleasant subject for a nice afternoon.'

He was quiet for a while, thinking, and then he said, 'I understand; if you met Cathy on that course, then you must have recently split up with somebody.'

I smiled. 'Good guess.'

'And you moved here to make a new start.'

'Another good guess.'

'Well,' he said, taking my hand exactly the way Ben had just done, 'I'm very glad you chose to move here, Carla. In fact, I think it was the perfect choice.'

I don't expect you'll be surprised to learn that I stayed for dinner. However, since you think I'm so bad with children, you might be surprised to hear that I put Ben to bed and read him a story. And that he insisted on kissing me good night.

After we'd eaten and Ben was asleep, Pete and I went back outside with our glasses of wine to sit on the blanket. It was dark, and the stars were just coming out. My original motives for seeking Pete out were long forgotten. At that moment, sitting close to Pete on the blanket under the stars, revenge was definitely the very last thing on my mind.

Yes, you've guessed it: if anything was on my mind just then, I suppose it was romance. Crazy, I know. After all, I'd only known Pete for a few hours. But somehow it wasn't as crazy as you'd think. Because Pete wasn't like Alec or Terry. He was young, attractive and above all nice. And I was hungry for nice, after you. And it's very, very lonely having to be strong all the time, believe me. Always having to keep a part of me secret.

And yet, of course, there was a barrier in the way of Pete and me getting together. Cathy.

Chapter 12 *Poetry and passion*

I think I knew, even then, that I didn't intend to carry out any acts of revenge on Pete. Out there on the blanket in the dark, sleepy garden, I encouraged him to talk about the past. I think I wanted to be convinced that he was a good man. That he deserved to live.

'Tell me,' I said. 'Tell me about your ghosts.'

He looked at me. 'You mean Cathy?' he asked, and then he sighed and lay down on the blanket with his eyes closed. For a while I thought he wasn't going to make any further response, but then he began to speak, and his voice was sad with remembered pain. 'I don't know what she's told you,' he said, 'but I'm not the big bad monster in all of this, honestly I'm not. When I first met Cathy, I loved her very much. We were so happy, and we got married really quickly.' He sighed heavily. 'I really believed it would last forever.' He paused there, but I didn't fill the waiting silence with questions and he soon continued with his story.

'Unfortunately, after we'd been married for a few years, Cathy became depressed. Seriously depressed. I did all I could to try and help her, but I felt completely inadequate. Nothing I did seemed to make any difference at all. So when she said she thought she'd feel better if we had children, I wasn't sure. But she begged me and begged me and finally I agreed. I suppose I should have known it wouldn't help, but as I said, I loved her. All I wanted was for her to be happy again. To have the Cathy I'd first met back again.'

'So it didn't help at all when Ben was born?' I asked, and Pete shook his head.

'No,' he said sadly, 'quite the opposite. She was even more depressed than ever.' And he went on to describe the desperate years of coping with Cathy's periods of depression. The times in hospital and the different doctors. The trials with various drugs. The attempts to kill herself. What he described seemed like a catalogue of despair and false hopes.

'I know you're a friend of Cathy's, Carla,' Pete said to me at last, 'but the truth is, I did all I could for her. She was completely unpredictable, and it simply wasn't safe to leave Ben alone with her. So I couldn't work. We were desperately poor, and although I knew Cathy was ill, I didn't feel she was really trying to help herself.'

'So, eventually you left?'

He nodded. 'Yes, eventually I left. But I assure you, it was the hardest thing I've ever had to do. But I had to think of Ben. And funnily enough, although I know Cathy's found it difficult since I left, I think she has been making more of an effort. She joined that course where she met you for a start, and now she's got a circle of friends. She's got her part-time job too.'

I didn't make any comment about this, and he sighed again, accurately interpreting my silence. 'Cathy's told you about my decision to cut payments to her, hasn't she?' he said, and I nodded.

'She's very worried about how she's going to manage,' I said.

'I know she is,' Pete said, sounding miserable. 'But the thing is, I'm just not going to be able to afford her payments any longer. I'm going back to university soon, to study creative writing. I've always dreamed of being a writer, and after so many years of looking after other people, I want to do something for myself. Is that so very selfish of me?'

I glanced up and found him looking at me intensely, his dark eyes demanding an answer. Perhaps even approval. 'Is that so selfish of me, Carla?' he repeated. '*Is* it?'

And do you know, somehow I found myself shaking my head. 'No,' I said, 'I don't think it is.'

Well, you know how I've always been interested in literature. And anyway, there was a bond of sympathy between us, a common understanding. We were connected by the experience of despair, and we were both survivors. Besides, the moon was shining down on the garden from over the trees and the sky above us was filled with a million stars. We were lying next to each other on a blanket beneath those stars, our shoulders touching. There had been an unspoken attraction between us right from the very start, and I know that if Ben hadn't woken up from a nightmare at that very moment, that attraction would have been acknowledged. We would have kissed, I know we would.

But as it was, Pete went indoors to comfort his son and by the time he came down again the moment had passed.

'Come out sailing with us tomorrow, Carla,' Pete said, squeezing my hands in his. 'Ben would love to see you again and . . . so would I.'

I blushed at that, and I don't think I ever did that with

you. Pete had such a warm, intense way of looking at me, it made me feel wanted. Needed. And it was a very long time since I'd truly felt either of those things.

Being with you was always so complex somehow. It was either fantastic or awful, depending on your mood. But Pete was different, and I think I sensed that difference straight away. I knew I would be able to wake up next to him in the morning and feel confident that he was the same man I'd gone to sleep next to the night before.

So I blushed and I smiled at him and I said, 'Thank you. I'd love to go sailing with you.'

And he smiled back and said, 'Good.'

I'll always remember that first day Pete, Ben and I went sailing on the Norfolk Broads. It was a truly perfect day. The weather was lovely, with not a cloud in the sky. Pete was an expert sailor, and little Ben seemed to be an equally expert helper, despite his age. There was nothing for me to do but sit and enjoy the view. And it was a very fine view, with tall grass and wild flowers on the river bank, and water birds swimming next to us.

When I wasn't looking at the view, I watched Ben and his father together, admiring how they worked as a team. Pete had a way of giving Ben tasks to do that made the boy feel important, and it was such a contrast to the way Cathy treated Ben. Cathy seemed to want Ben to be dependent upon her. She treated him more like a baby than an intelligent, capable young boy, and as a result he behaved like a baby. More than once I'd seen Ben really lose his temper when he'd been with Cathy, shouting and crying and stamping his foot when he didn't get his own way about something.

But that day on the boat he was very different.

'Daddy, there's a man selling ice creams!' he said once, pointing at the river bank. 'Can I have one?'

'Not just now, son. It's nearly lunch time. An ice cream will spoil your appetite. You can have one later.'

And Ben gave the ice cream man one final look then started to play with a piece of rope which was lying on the deck.

'I'm impressed,' I told Pete. 'If Cathy had tried to say that to him, he'd have gone mad.'

'But she wouldn't have said it, would she?' Pete pointed out. 'She'd have let him have the ice cream and then wondered why he didn't want to eat any lunch.'

It was true, I had to admit, and I couldn't help thinking, as I sat there on the boat with the sun on my face and a soft wind in my hair, that your daughters would have benefited a lot from such an approach. You spoilt them by giving them everything they wanted whenever they asked for it.

At lunch time we tied the boat up at a picnic area and ate sandwiches and fruit. Afterwards Ben ran around entertaining himself by chasing butterflies, and Pete and I chatted about the course he was about to start at university. He told me that he'd always written stories and poems, and that poetry had been his lifeline during the long unhappy years with Cathy.

'Everyone needs to be able to express themselves, don't they?' he said. 'I've always loved finding out about writers, and reading their books. It's fascinating. The times I've got into trouble for reading when I shouldn't be reading! At work, even on my honeymoon! I can't seem to help it. If

I see an interesting piece of writing, I've started reading before I know it. And now I've got the chance to become a writer myself! It's fantastic!'

We were sitting on a blanket again, this time beneath some willow trees. The long branches were moving about in the wind, making sunshine patterns on Pete's face as he spoke. Dappled shade, just like in our garden when you told me it was all over. And yet, that afternoon with Pete, I can't honestly remember thinking about you or how you so brutally ended our relationship at all. I was just enjoying being with Pete, admiring his enthusiasm, appreciating the brightness in his eyes.

That day on the river bank, you were just a vague misty memory. And so was my very recent past. Don't you think the mind is a strange thing? To some extent it can select what you remember.

Until something happens to make sure you face up to the truth.

'I want to know more about you,' Pete was saying. 'People are so fascinating to me, but particularly you. I want to know all your likes and dislikes. I know, let's start with poetry; it's something very close to my own heart. What's your favourite poem?'

I was able to answer straight away. '"Summer with Monica" by Roger McGough.'

He smiled, reaching out to stroke the hair from my face. 'Ah,' he said, 'a love story.' And then he leaned over and . . . he kissed me.

That kiss was as gentle as one of Ben's butterflies would have felt if it had landed on my mouth. And yet it set off a fierce storm of desire in both me and Pete.

We pulled apart and looked at each other. I think we were both a little shocked by the force of our feelings.

'Maybe we should slow down,' Pete told me softly.

I looked into his face, and I suppose I probably looked worried because he reached out to touch my cheek.

'I like you, Carla,' he said. 'I like you a lot. I don't want to rush into things and spoil them. Let's keep things special, yes?'

When you first told me our relationship was over, I felt as if I would never recover. I didn't know who I was or what I was going to do. But there in Pete's arms, with him smiling down at me and talking about keeping things special, I found myself again.

'Yes,' I said. 'Let's keep things special.' And I felt happy and sad at the same time. Happy, because Pete accepted me exactly as I was. And sad because he would never, ever, know exactly what I was like.

Because how could I ever tell him he was holding a double murderer in his arms?

Chapter 13 *Hot water*

For the next two weeks, I only returned to my flat once to fetch some clothes. The three of us went out on the boat on fine days, which was nearly every day. And in the evenings, Pete and I talked, cooked each other meals and kissed.

In the middle of the second week Cathy came to collect Ben, to take him to stay with her for a few days. I kept upstairs out of the way while Cathy was there. It seemed the least complicated option, somehow. And as I lay on the bed with the bedroom door open, I listened to Cathy talking to Pete.

'Nobody knows where my friend Carla's gone,' Cathy said. 'She's just disappeared. It isn't like her to go off like that, not without telling anybody. And Gemma's going half crazy trying to organise a funeral and a wedding. It's taken the police a while to release her husband's body, and they still haven't got a clue who killed him. And Diane's had to go to Cuba to sort everything out over there. Carla was the only one of us who hadn't had anything dramatic happen to her, and now she's gone and disappeared —'

'Look, Cathy,' I heard Pete interrupt her. 'I'm going to have to ask you to go. I've got an appointment to get to.' I noticed that Pete sounded different talking to Cathy. When he spoke to me, his voice was soft and unhurried, as if he had all the time in the world. But when he spoke to Cathy, there was a distinct edge of impatience to his voice.

Cathy was clearly annoyed at being cut off in full flow. 'Well, pardon me for wasting your valuable time!' she said angrily.

'Don't be like that, Cathy,' Pete said, obviously doing his best to be more patient. 'It's just that I'm really busy today.'

'Too busy to speak to the mother of your child, I suppose!' Cathy went on. 'Too busy to discuss how I'm going to afford to buy food when you cut off your payments!'

'I'll see what I can do about the payments,' I heard Pete say tiredly, and Cathy's voice immediately changed.

'You'll carry on with them?' she said excitedly. 'Really? Do you promise?'

'I'll try,' Pete replied. 'That's all I can say. Now, I really must get ready.'

Their voices became more distant and I guessed they were heading towards the front door.

'You've got an interview, haven't you?' I heard Cathy guess wrongly. 'You've got an interview and you've given up the idea of going to university!'

After he'd finally got rid of her, Pete came upstairs and collapsed onto the bed beside me. 'Don't say anything!' He warned me, half joking. 'I know I'm weak, but I just couldn't stand another one of her moods, that's all.'

I put my arms around him and we lay together in comfortable silence for a while. Then, after he'd calmed down, he looked at me. 'Your friends lead dramatic lives, don't they?' he observed. 'Two murders in the space of two weeks.'

'And one unexplained disappearance!' I joked, hoping to change the subject.

Pete laughed. 'Would you like to disappear with me forever?' he asked, kissing the side of my neck, and the thing is, I wanted to say yes. I was so happy being around Pete. He made me feel totally safe and loved, in a way you never did.

'Yes,' I said. 'Let's do it!'

He seemed astonished, pulling back to look at me. 'Do what?' he asked.

'Disappear,' I said. 'Make a new start somewhere else. Somewhere where nobody knows us!' I think I probably sounded a bit too eager, even perhaps a little desperate, because he looked at me strangely.

'Well,' he said after a while, 'I can't, can I? There's Ben to consider. And Cathy. She might be a bit of a pain, but she is his mother. I can't deny him his mother. Besides, there's my university course . . . '

I did my best to smile, recovering as quickly as possible. I could tell from his reaction that my voice had probably sounded dangerously similar to Cathy's. 'Of course there is,' I said. 'You're right. It was just a silly idea.'

'Are you sure?' he asked, sounding concerned. 'You seemed . . . Is everything all right, Carla?'

I laughed, and to my relief the laugh sounded quite normal. 'I'm fine!' I assured him. 'Fine. As I said, it was just a silly idea. Now, are you going to lie there talking all afternoon or are you going to make love to me?'

He smiled at that and started to kiss me, but although I responded, for the first time since we'd been together I didn't really experience much pleasure from our passion. I was filled with too much regret.

And I thought about you, for the first time in days. With

hatred. Because it was your fault that I had secrets I needed to keep from the man I loved. Your fault that I was a murderer.

Life carried on as normal for the next few days. Pete's holidays were over and he had to go back to work. I knew I should look for a new job myself; my savings weren't going to last forever. But somehow I didn't feel motivated to buy a newspaper or visit the Job Centre. I don't think I realised it at the time, but looking back now I think I was feeling very uncertain about what the future might bring. And quite rightly so.

Because one afternoon I came back from a peaceful walk around the lake at Whitlingham to find that Pete was already home. And the first thing I saw when I let myself in through the back door, was . . . this notebook, lying open on the kitchen table.

I think my heart stopped. I know I couldn't breathe properly and I had to grab hold of the kitchen table to stop myself from falling. I stood there for a long time, staring at the open book and holding on to the table, my body frozen by horror. I didn't leave it there like that. Did I? I know I was sitting there writing, but I put it back in my bag. Surely I did. He wouldn't have taken it out of my bag. Would he? The words crashed around inside my head, over and over again. And suddenly I remembered our conversation about reading when we'd been sitting on the river bank, the first time we'd gone out in the boat. 'The times I've got into trouble for reading when I shouldn't be reading!' Pete had said. 'At work, even on my honeymoon! I can't seem to help it. If I see an interesting piece of writing, I've started reading before I know it.'

Eventually my limbs must have unlocked, I suppose, because I managed to move over to the book to look down at the open pages, trying to see what he'd been reading. I kept having to blink because my eyes wouldn't focus properly. Maybe I was crying, I don't know. I only know that at first my hand-written words in the notebook swam around in front of my eyes, making no sense to me.

But when, at last, the words became steady enough to make sense, I could see that the book wasn't open at the page I had been writing on. And one word, in particular, leapt straight out from the page at me.

Weedkiller.

I'm not sure what I would have done if Pete hadn't chosen that exact moment to call down to me from upstairs. Maybe I would just have grabbed my book and run away. Disappeared out of Pete's life forever. Moved abroad. Had plastic surgery to change my identity.

But he did call down to me.

'Carla? I'm up here, in the bath! Come and join me; I've got something I want to talk to you about!'

I didn't stop to analyse the sound of his voice; I was totally convinced he was going to ask me about the notebook. To accuse me of murder.

As I made my way slowly up the stairs, listening to the sound of Pete in the bath, I had no idea of what I was going to do. I didn't go up there with the intention of killing him, I really didn't. To be honest, I didn't even feel I was inhabiting my body properly. It was as if I was floating somewhere above myself, watching with curiosity as I reached the top of the stairs.

There was a small electric fire on the landing with a long

cable. I bent to plug it in and picked it up carefully, walking with it towards the open door of the bathroom. Then I threw it into the bathwater with Pete.

Chapter 14   *Tidying up*

Prison is a very boring place. Oh, they give you work to do; you have a job. But you don't exactly receive careers advice or get to choose the job you want. Choice doesn't come into it; you do what you're told.

They told me to clean the kitchens, so that's what I do. Every day. My hands are red and rough, and my skin is white from being indoors so much. And I've only been here two months.

But I'd better put you right; you'll be thinking I've been arrested and locked up for murder. No, that's not what happened at all. The truth is much harder to believe. During the long hours I'm locked up in my cell I think to myself, 'If only I knew a writer; if only I could tell a writer my story. It would be a best-selling book . . .'

But of course I get depressed when I start to think things like that. Because I did know a writer. And I killed him.

I screamed after I'd thrown the fire into the bath. Screamed and screamed and screamed, with my hands over my ears. I didn't realise it was me doing the screaming at first. As soon as I did, I stopped. But the tears were still pouring down my face, and I was groaning like an injured animal.

It was just the same as in the kitchen: I was paralysed again, completely unable to move. Only this time, instead of my open book, I was standing there staring at the face of my dead lover. A face turned ugly by death.

There was a magazine in the water, a magazine Pete had been reading before he died. A travel brochure. As I stared at it, the significance of its presence in the bath sent a wave of pure terror sweeping right through me.

And suddenly I was running. Away from the murder scene. Along the landing. Down the stairs. But no matter how fast I ran, I couldn't escape my thoughts.

Why would Pete have been reading a travel brochure in the bath if he was about to accuse me of murder?

In the kitchen, I reached for my notebook, my eyes desperately travelling over the lines of writing. 'Gardening is very relaxing for me.' I read. Luis's words, in his little garden. 'Yes; out here I have only the weeds to fight. And I have a good friend to help me to do that. My weedkiller. It is very strong, Those weeds, they have not got a chance.'

I quickly turned the pages, searching for my account of Alec Cartwright's murder. I had to turn quite a few pages before I reached it. And suddenly it was difficult to breathe. Suddenly I knew that it was quite possible I had just made the biggest, most heartbreaking mistake of my entire life. That it was quite possible Pete hadn't known anything about my murders at all.

I didn't stop to think about any evidence or clues I might have left in the house. I did hurry around, collecting what clothes and possessions I could see, but I didn't wipe any objects I might have touched. I was far too upset to think in such a logical way. I had just murdered the man I loved, and I needed to escape.

Except, of course, that there was no escape. There is never any escape. Especially at night, when I lie awake in the darkness and I see Pete's dead eyes staring back at me from the bath. But as I ran from Pete's house, I don't think I quite realised just how impossible it was going to be to escape.

I ran to my car and drove off, my tyres screaming. I didn't even return to my house. Why would I? There was nothing for me there any more. So I just drove and drove. I didn't even make the decision to drive north; it just turned out that way. And apart from getting petrol, I didn't stop.

I didn't even know I was heading towards Whitby until I saw the first road sign. Why did I choose Whitby, I wonder? Our place? How was it possible that, even then, after everything that had just happened, I was still thinking about you? Because Whitby was the place we went to for a romantic holiday soon after we met. Our special place. A place for walking hand in hand on the windswept sands and eating fish and chips on the harbour wall.

But I didn't walk on the sands or eat fish and chips this time, because I was involved in a car crash before I got there. On the A1, to be precise, just south of York. The driver of the other vehicle was a well-dressed woman in her fifties, and when I got out of my car to inspect the damage, she began to shout at me. Accusing me of dangerous driving. Threatening me with her solicitor. And suddenly I'd had enough so . . . I hit her.

I hit her very hard. And while she was recovering, I hit her again. And again. When she fell to the ground, I kicked her. And who knows what else I might have done, but at some point a lorry driver grabbed me and kept hold of me until the police arrived.

But I don't suppose I need to tell you all of this, do I? You must know about it. Just about everybody in the whole of England knows about it. Because the aggressive woman was a politician, and her picture – and mine – appeared on the front of just about every newspaper in the country. And on television. Quite a coincidence, wasn't it? Out of all the thousands and thousands of drivers on the A1 that evening, I had to be involved in an accident with her.

When I look at that picture now; her with her cut, bruised face and me staring straight at the camera, I hardly recognise myself. There's no conscience in my face at all. No sign of regret or shame. Well, I didn't feel either regret or shame, and I couldn't pretend otherwise. That's why I got such a long sentence, I think.

'Such displays of senseless aggression cannot be allowed to go unpunished,' the judge concluded at the court case. 'It is this court's intention to make an example of you. I therefore sentence you to the maximum term for such a crime. You will go to prison for two years.'

In my mind, however, I'm in prison for life. Because surely it's only a matter of time before the investigations by the police into those three separate unsolved murders lead them in my direction. And in some ways, it will be a relief. Except that, if I do stay in prison for the rest of my life, then nothing will ever happen to you. You'll bring up your spoilt girls to be spoilt young women and you'll forget that you ever had a girlfriend called Carla.

*   *   *

The most wonderful thing has happened! I had three visitors this afternoon! Can you guess who?

Actually, when the guard first told me I had visitors, I was expecting them to be the police. Either that or some boring relative. But it was Diane, Gemma and Cathy. The girls!

I was so pleased to see some friendly faces that I forgot, for a moment, that they might not be friendly. I had, after all, murdered their ex-husbands.

'You all look so good!' I said, and it was true. All three of them were dressed smartly with styled hair and perfect make-up. They could have stepped straight from the pages of a fashion magazine.

'I can't say the same about you, I'm afraid,' Diane said, and I blushed with sudden embarrassment, my hand going up to my unwashed hair.

'There doesn't seem much point in making an effort in here,' I said softly, and Diane shook her head.

'No,' she said, 'I don't suppose there does.'

There was a silence then, and I could feel each one of them looking at me. Hard. It didn't come as too much of a surprise when Gemma finally said, 'We know, Carla. We know what you did.'

I suppose I could have tried to deny it, but suddenly I didn't have the energy any longer. 'I'm sorry,' I said, and I looked down at my rough red hands, feeling ashamed. There was another silence, and this time I risked looking up. All three of them were still staring at me as if I were an object on display in an exhibition. 'How . . . how did you find out?' I asked.

'We asked questions, talked to people, drew conclusions,' Diane said.

'We guessed a lot of it,' Gemma added.

'Ben told me you were at Pete's,' Cathy said.

I reacted at the mention of his name; I couldn't help it. But they didn't seem to notice, or if they did, then they assumed I was reacting out of fear, not out of heartbreak.

'So after Cathy found the body,' Diane said, whispering now, 'she called us, and we went round and did a thorough cleaning job before we phoned the police.'

I stared at them, feeling completely confused, and Gemma suddenly burst out laughing. 'We're grateful to you!' she said. 'All of us!'

'Very grateful,' Diane agreed.

'But — ' I started to say, but she interrupted me.

'I know I was upset at first. Well, that was before I went over to Cuba and met your friend Luis. He made me face up to what my husband was really like. Lovely man, Luis. He asked after you, by the way; sent you his love. If I were you, I'd get myself back over to Cuba the minute they set you free from this place!'

'I'm rich!' Gemma continued with a huge smile. 'As our divorce still wasn't final, I inherited all his money. Kirsty had the most wonderful wedding. You should have seen her, Carla. Oh, she looked beautiful! There was even a feature about it in Hi Society Magazine!'

'And I've got my little boy living with me all the time,' Cathy said.

Instantly I was in Pete's garden in Trowse, watching little Ben playing at ice cream monsters with his father. And I thought of you. You who had first planted those seeds of murder in my heart with your cruelty. You who were at that very moment in time, living your life happily in the house which was once my home too.

'So, what we want to know,' Diane was saying, 'is what we can do to show you how grateful we are.'

'Yes,' Gemma agreed. 'If there's anything we can do, Carla, just name it.'

'Anything at all,' Cathy said. 'Anything.'

I was still thinking of you when I started to smile at them. It was the first thing I'd smiled about since Pete had died.

'Yes,' I said. 'There is something you can do for me. Some rubbish you can get rid of for me.'

Then I began to laugh.

Cambridge English Readers

Look out for other titles at level 6:

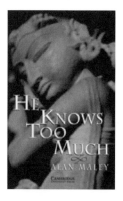

He Knows Too Much
Alan Maley

An English company executive in India is dismissed after he tries to uncover corruption within his company. He returns to England where his life falls apart and his marriage breaks up. He then sets out on a one-man search for the truth behind his dismissal. He turns to the rich mystery and beauty of India and is finally forced to choose between love and revenge.

Deadly Harvest
Carolyn Walker

Chief Inspector Jane Honeywell is a city detective who wonders why she has moved to a sleepy country town – nothing happens in Pilton. But then the rural peace and quiet is suddenly disturbed by a horrible murder. When Jane starts the dangerous pursuit of the killer, she discovers a more terrible plan in operation.

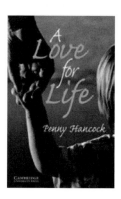

A Love for Life
Penny Hancock

In Cambridge, Fanella bravely faces the challenge of adopting a child alone after her partner leaves her. Fanella and five-year-old Ellie get off to a rocky start, but Fanella patiently steers their relationship onto more solid ground. Meanwhile, her relationship with Rod, Ellie's teacher and a married man, is a little more complicated.

Frozen Pizza and other slices of life
Antoinette Moses

A collection of stories that offer eight slices of life in England today. The themes covered include British eating habits, the media, inner-city problems, immigration, football hooliganism, student life, leisure activities, and the countryside. Well-observed, lively, and amusing, these stories provide a fascinating picture of the country at the start of a new century.

This Time It's Personal
Alan Battersby

Private Investigator Nathan Marley takes thing personally as he tries to prove the innocence of murder suspect, José – a member of his assistant Stella's family. The search for proof takes him into the heart of the New York Russian American community as unidentified bodies are washed up on a beach. Marley must work fast to save José and find the real culprits.

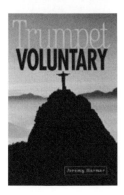

Trumpet Voluntary
Jeremy Harmer

A musician disappears leaving only a strange e-mail message. Her husband, in a desperate search to find her, revisits their shared past and has to face up to some unpleasant realities, before trying to rebuild his life. His journey of discovery takes us across the world to Poland and Rio and deep into the human heart.

The *Cambridge Advanced Learner's Dictionary* provides a clear, reliable guide to modern English. This new edition, based on the 600 million words Cambridge International Corpus, has been completely updated and redesigned.

The CD-ROM provides special tools to help with writing, pronunciation and vocabulary building.

find words easily!

- 80,000 words and phrases with over 10,000 phrasal verbs and idioms
- Idiom finder: a simple way to find complicated idioms

choose words quickly!

- Guidewords help you choose the right meaning
- Simple definitions
- Over 1,000 words explained in pictures

use words correctly!

- Over 90,000 example sentences
- Common learner errors help you avoid mistakes
- Over 25,000 collocations

Take a tour! Visit *dictionary.cambridge.org/cald*